to Dad
from Luke

I Love my
Dad !!!!!!! \ \ \ !!. Love
Luke

5/26/9

BRETT FAVRE

BRETT FAVRE

HUCK FINN GROWS UP

Steve Cameron

MASTERS PRESS

A Division of Howard W. Sams & Company
A Bell Atlantic Company

Published by Masters Press
A Division of Howard W. Sams & Company,
A Bell Atlantic Company
2647 Waterfront Pkwy E. Dr, Suite 300, Indianapolis, IN 46214

Printed in the United States of America.

96 97 98 99 00 01   10 9 8 7 6 5 4 3 2 1

Library of Congress Cataloging-in-Publication Data

Cameron, Steve.
        Brett Favre: Huck Finn Grows Up / Steve Cameron
            p.   cm.
        ISBN 1-57028-112-2 (cloth)
        1. Favre, Brett. 2. Football players -- United States --
Biography. 3. Green Bay Packers (Football team)-- History.
4. Quarterback (Football) I. Title.

GV939.F29C35   1996   96-41476
[B]   CIP

For Margaret, Michael and Jane, who have been wondering why I spend so much time hogging the computer.

TABLE OF CONTENTS

ACKNOWLEDGEMENTS

This is the third time I've written a book centered around the Green Bay Packers franchise, and again I find myself amazed at how friendly and cooperative everyone connected with that organization can be — even when faced with the blizzard of demands that come with being one of pro football's elite teams.

From the top on down, everyone in the Packer family was wonderful to us, and it would have been impossible to do the project justice without them: president Bob Harlan, general manager Ron Wolf, coach Mike Holmgren and my sage ol' pal, public relations director Lee Remmel, along with his entire staff.

Our receptions in Wisconsin and Mississippi were astounding, in part because Brett Favre has so many friends but also because these are genuinely nice people.

The list of thanks must start with the Favre family, which greeted me warmly at their home in Fenton (not Kiln) and not only encouraged access to Brett's most personal pieces of history but introduced me to a fabulous Gulf Coast tradition, red beans and rice for lunch on Mondays. To

Irvin and Bonita Favre, their sons Scott and Jeff and daughter Brandi, gratitude isn't a strong enough word. The same can be said of the former Deanna Tynes — now Mrs. Brett Favre — who was warm and gracious even at a time when Brett was just beginning his difficult treatment program for painkiller addiction. All of these kind folks personify southern hospitality.

Several of Brett's current and former teammates were good enough to share time and tales, as well. It's a long list, but the players who made a special effort include Frank Winters, Mark Chmura and Robbie Weeks. And Lynn Dickey, a great Packer quarterback in his own right, provided astounding insight not only into Favre's skills but also the pains and pressures which can lead to the addiction Favre endured.

Everyone involved with this book also received red-carpet treatment from the athletic department at the University of Southern Mississippi — notably sports information director Regiel Napier and three members of the current football staff: Jeff Bower, Mark McHale and Thamus Coleman.

Some people did specialized research to help see this project through, and they deserve a particularly deep bow: Chuck Carlson of the *Appleton Post-Crescent* and his wife Theresa, along with Al Jones and Doug Barber of the *Sun Herald* in the Gulfport.

Snippets, anecdotes and some quotations were culled from various magazines, newspapers and other publications too numerous to mention. But I recognize the work of my colleagues in the media and trust I've kept their material in the proper perspective.

On the photo side, we're indebted once again to Vernon Biever, the Packers' official photographer for nearly 40 years; Tim Isbell of the *Sun Herald* and, one more time, the Southern Miss athletic department.

This is my first book for Masters Press, and the gang there has been helpful, supportive and professional every step of the way. Without the faith of Tom Bast and the day-to-day encouragement of editor Holly Kondras, it could never have happened.

Thanks also, to longtime buddy Jeff Flanagan, who first suggested the idea for this book; to my agent Bob Snodgrass, who handled all the grubby paperwork so I could do the fun stuff; and to the rest of the gang in Kansas City who kept me going when things got tough — Gib Twyman, Tim Keithley and Bob Casey.

I would be remiss, as well, if I didn't nod in the direction of the *Charleston Gazette*, and particularly sports editor Mitch Vingle, for giving me the time to finish this book before starting our season coverage of West Virginia football.

My wife, Sylvia, not only suffered through a cloud of cigar smoke while I was working, she turned out to be a first-rate proofreader in addition to keeping me supplied with Diet Coke, cranberry muffins and a world of loving help. In fact, you would read Syl's name on the dedication page, except that she's holding out for special mention in my first novel.

And finally, thanks a hundred times over to Brett Favre, a great football player and even better guy. It's saying something when you spend six months prying into the life of a professional athlete and can't find anyone who doesn't like him.

Amazing. But that's why Brett is Brett in the first place, and why we did this book.

FOREWORD

I'm a Brett Favre fan.

A lot of people have heard me say that — in conversations, interviews and public appearances. Perhaps they make the obvious connection that my ties to the Green Bay Packers, for whom I played and coached, remain so strong that I certainly would be pulling for any Packer quarterback.

They're right, up to a point, but my appreciation for Brett and the challenges this young man has faced go beyond any simple allegiance to my old team and those years of wonderful memories.

I can appreciate the fight, the toughness and the competitive fire in Brett Favre. It's easy to say that now, of course, since he's become the league's Most Valuable Player and led the Packers to the NFC championship game. However, Brett had to be a battler just to crack the Green Bay lineup. He was buried in the No. 3 job as a rookie in Atlanta and was almost completely untested when an injury to starter Don Majkowski gave him a chance to play in 1992.

Even before that, Brett had conquered long odds just to reach the NFL. He barely got a scholarship out of high school, and then just when his college career at Southern Miss was taking off, he had to endure the effects of a terrible auto accident that left him weak his entire senior year.

Clearly, Brett was not handed the stardom he has enjoyed the past couple of years.

It's tough to believe strongly in your own ability, while being forced to endure a backup or substitute role. It's frustrating to know your future in the NFL might be in doubt.

In that situation, you must keep working, learning, and persist with a great attitude and self-confidence. Those traits are even more important for a quarterback who, if he eventually gets a chance to play, will be judged on leadership and mental strength as much as on his skills throwing the football.

Brett Favre has passed all of these tests.

He hung in there through the disappointing year in Atlanta, prepared himself to play in Green Bay and rallied the Packers the moment he got a chance. Even in subsequent years, when Brett was still maturing as a quarterback and made some predictable mistakes, he fought off criticism and whatever self-doubt crops up in the wake of sub-par performances.

In short, Brett developed himself into a complete professional after beginning at the end of the bench, and having traveled that same road myself, I truly appreciate his effort.

Brett's assets/talents are impressive. No one possesses more courage, toughness or tenacity. Combine these with a rocket arm, good mobility, strength and supreme confidence and you have an exceptionally talented young quarterback. To Ron Wolf's credit, he saw these qualities in Brett and thus traded for him. What a move!!

Now, of course, Brett faces yet another challenge as he attempts to put the curse of painkiller addiction behind him to get on with his career and, more important, with his life.

Nothing I've seen in this young man indicates that he will fail himself, his wonderful family or his teammates. If anyone is mentally prepared to win a tough battle, it's Brett Favre.

Even as we all enjoy Brett's remarkable story as chronicled in this book, even as we watch his emergence as one of the most thrilling quarterbacks of this or any other era, we all should pray and pull for him in the larger game of life.

I think his success, both on and off the field, will dramatically increase. He's a remarkable talent who is truly blessed with a great family and support system. Additionally, we all know that Brett is a fighter.

Besides, as stated before, I'm a Brett Favre fan. A huge one!

Bart Starr
August, 1996

BRETT FAVRE

HUCK FINN GROWS UP

INTRODUCTION

Your quarterback is a different kind of cat.

Just ask John Madden, America's most famous coach-turned-broadcaster. Madden considers himself something of an expert on the personality traits exhibited by certain types of athletes. He claims, for instance, that he can spot a linebacker in a shopping mall just from one peek at his eyes.

Don't sell Madden short here, either.

I took a cross-country train with Big John a few years ago, and when the westbound California Zephyr stopped at Laramie, Wyoming, a group of relatively tall and graceful-looking young ladies stepped on board. It didn't take Madden — or the two sports writers traveling with him — terribly long to guess that the newcomers had to be the University of Wyoming women's basketball team.

Perhaps an hour out of Laramie, our little group happened to be in the dining car when the lady hoopsters came walking in. Along with a couple of coaches and a team manager, they filled up several tables at the other end of the diner.

1

Madden proposed a bet. Each of the three of us, he suggested, would write down on a napkin which of these Wyoming players were the team's five starters. Remember, none of us had ever seen them before, and the rules of the bet stipulated that we could walk over to where the team was sitting and say hello, but no questions were allowed. In other words, we had to guess the starters just from watching them eat dinner.

I was fairly amazed that I managed to pick three starters out of the crowd. The other journalist on our junket also got three correct — the same trio I'd selected. But Madden, unbelievably, got all five right.

Wonder why he was a great coach? John spent just a few minutes looking at 12 women from, oh, 25 feet away and effectively scouted out the whole team. When we told the Wyoming coaches what we'd done, they were amazed, since one of the girls — a freshman who was very shy and had barely said a word during the meal — only had been installed as a starter a couple of weeks earlier.

You can see why I put a decent amount of stock in Madden's analysis of athletes, and most certainly his reading of football players.

"Quarterbacks aren't like anybody else," Madden once said. "They're the guys who, when they were in third or fourth grade and all the kids were first starting to choose up teams at recess, they just took over and said, 'Bobby and I will be captains and pick teams. I'll take Billy.'

"You don't want to get into any kind of a game with a quarterback. These are the kind of people who can beat you in golf, tiddly-winks, racquetball, Monopoly or pitching pennies. They pitch and play shortstop in baseball, and make all the big shots with the crowd screaming in basketball. They're natural-born heroes. You teach 'em a new game, and in an hour, they can beat you at it. Quarterbacks are good at everything, and from the time they're old enough to talk you out of your turkey sandwich at lunchtime, they never lose.

"Quarterbacks are always teacher's pets, and they go with the prettiest girls, and the class genius with Coke-bottle glasses will always help them with their homework. Everybody is jealous of quarterbacks, because they're always the coolest guys in school."

But Madden's most important observation about quarterbacks was this: They *know* they're the best and they expect to win — all the time. Quarterbacks, he insists, are as fearless as they are talented, and the best ones truly believe themselves to be bulletproof.

Now, I wasn't around when Brett Favre was in grade school or when he played for his daddy, Irvin, at Hancock North Central High down near the Mississippi Gulf Coast. I saw Brett in a couple of all-star games following his college career, but I never met him in person until the summer of 1993, when I was writing a 75th-anniversary commemorative book about the Green Bay Packers.

I'll say this, though: After one conversation with Brett Lorenzo Favre — at that time beginning his third year of professional football — I flashed back instantly to John Madden's description of a guy who was born to play quarterback.

Brett was that guy.

And the more you think about it, Madden's quarterback profile goes a long way toward explaining a lot of the thrilling highs and terrifying lows that Favre, still just 26, has experienced both in his life and his career.

Don't be fooled by the happy-go-lucky attitude and the aw-shucks demeanor he brought out of the bayou country: Brett Favre thinks he's invincible. He can scramble for any first down, find a receiver when everybody's covered, even survive auto accidents and the wallop of dangerous pharmaceuticals.

For a superstar quarterback, it goes with the territory.

How could this kid who threw an average of five passes a game in high school be so cock-sure that he could be a big-time thrower in college?

He was.

How could he stroll off the bench as a third-string freshman at Southern Mississippi and tell bruised, battle-tested linemen that it was time to rock and roll?

He did.

How in the world did he race into the huddle that first time in Green Bay — having never completed an NFL pass — and simply take over a team that had belonged to starter Don Majkowski?

He did that, too.

On the flip side, why doesn't Brett have any fear of risking life and limb? He had three feet of intestines removed in surgery after wrapping his car around a tree in college, and never doubted he'd come back, not only to play but shock mighty Alabama on the road just a few weeks later.

Quarterback to quarterback: TV analyst Joe Theismann
chats with Favre prior to a Sunday night game.

No matter how many interceptions he threw in that dizzying 1993 season — and some of 'em were outrageously bad — Favre always believed the next play would be a great one. When coaches screamed at him, he tuned it out because he was sure he'd save the day in the fourth quarter. Or next week. Or sometime.

Whenever Packers coach Mike Holmgren, occasionally driven to eye-rolling frustration by Favre's wild improvisations, would ask his young pupil if he was really, truly understanding the team's offensive concept, Brett always answered that he got it. But he'll tell you now that, shoot, sometimes the schemes seemed as confusing as translating the playbook from Arabic.

But a quarterback with the right stuff always believes he's got things under control. Or will have, maybe on the next series.

The same principle, I'm afraid, applies to the terrible bind that Brett eventually got himself into using painkillers. At first, he needed relief from injury because he *had* to be on the field. That's where leaders are supposed to be, rallying the troops instead of limping around on the sidelines.

When the insidious narcotic effect of Vicodin seized Favre in its grip and he began gobbling pills just to keep going from one day to the next, I suspect he always figured he could kick the stuff whenever he felt like it. That's the way quarterbacks think. Remember, they've spent their whole lives taking charge.

And now that Brett has handed himself over to doctors and counselors for treatment to put matters right, naturally he's positive he'll whip this demon just as he's learned to cope with fourth-quarter deficits and free-safety blitzes. What else could we expect?

I'll confess at the outset of this book that in addition to being fascinated by Brett Favre's rather remarkable story, I genuinely like the guy. That doesn't exactly make me the Lone Ranger, since everybody from the mayor of Green Bay to the Packers ball boys to the librarian back in Kiln, Mississippi, no doubt loves him to death.

The first time I set up an interview with Brett, for that Packers anniversary book back in '93, he was finishing up a mini-camp and preparing to leave town. I mean, right that second. He asked if we could talk on the phone, and if just a few minutes would be OK, since he had to catch a flight.

I really didn't have any choice, so I hauled out a notebook with my most important questions about the Packers' present and future listed on top, and started firing away. I've had years of experience doing these quickie sessions with sports stars, so I was prepared for the worst.

Get something good, right away. Get a decent response in the first two minutes, before this kid says: Sorry, gotta run.

So what happened is that I asked a general sort of question, just a warmup throw, and Brett proceeded to talk almost non-stop for an hour. I'm telling you, he could do monologues long enough to wear out the Energizer® bunny. Jay Leno and David Letterman would get exhausted trying to stitch great lines together like this kid.

I didn't need a notebook. I needed a binder thicker than Webster's Dictionary to scribble down everything Brett had to say about the Packers, about Green Bay, about the NFL, about the world in general.

And when he finally paused for breath, Brett said, "I hope that helps you out." I found out later that he'd been packing his suitcase and practically leaning out the front door while we'd been talking. I forgot to ask later if he missed his flight, but it wouldn't surprise me.

Back then, I suspected that the Pack was on an upswing and that Favre would develop into one of the league's impact quarterbacks. I'll confess I had no clue that he'd lead Green Bay's historic franchise back into the highest echelons of football — throwing 38 touchdown passes and snagging the 1995 MVP award along the way — or that his face would wind up gracing most of the country's major sports magazines.

I also had no idea that he'd fall into a dead-serious battle with painkiller addiction, either.

But even without any of that sort of fortune-telling, I was doggone sure of one thing in the spring of 1993: Meeting Brett Favre, I'd come across a once-in-a-lifetime kind of guy.

And that someday, I wanted to write a book about him.

When I told Brett, three years after our first chat and about a month before he volunteered himself for substance-abuse treatment, that this project indeed was coming to fruition, he laughed and wondered how I'd manage to re-create all those Mississippi accents in print. And he said he hoped I'd find enough to write about.

Not to worry, Brett.

Your story is so improbable, so entertaining, I'd probably have trouble selling it as fiction. Like a jockey riding a champion racehorse, all I have to do is sit still and not screw it up.

So hand me the reins and I promise not to fall off.

Steve Cameron
Charleston, West Virginia
August 1996

CHAPTER ONE:
WHAT, ME WORRY?

The first clue came early, when Brett Favre spotted a buddy in the back of the room and winked.

Oh, he'd tried to look serious and thoughtful for a minute which, given the situation, Brett probably thought would be appropriate. Here he was, after all, meeting the press for the first time since admitting two months earlier that he had developed an addiction to pain medication and would be entering a rehabilitation center.

Given Favre's status as reigning MVP in the National Football League, not to mention the continuous frenzy that surrounds the Green Bay Packers throughout their home state, it's questionable whether the President of the United States could have drawn a bigger media crowd than the mob that jammed seats, walls, railings, floor space and doorways in the Pack's downstairs auditorium at Lambeau Field on July 17, 1996.

Several local television stations, as well as ESPN, carried the press conference live. Hundreds of fans, denied admittance into the stadium, gathered faithfully in the parking lot — looking very much like anxious Catholics gathered in St. Peter's Square to await the election of a new pope.

Would there be white smoke or black smoke?

Figuratively speaking, that was what the public wanted to know about Favre, too. The last time anyone but family, a couple of close friends and coach Mike Holmgren had seen the Packer quarterback, he was standing grimly in the same auditorium, reading a statement about his problem and promising to go get well.

So Favre's reappearance in public was big stuff, and not just in Green Bay. Representatives of national media outlets turned out in force to hear what pro football's hottest young thrower had to say about his health, his career, his life.

What would he look like? How would he handle delicate questions about addiction? Might he aim darts at some of the NFL's pill-dispensing medical practices, which recently have come under serious scrutiny?

That business about how NFL teams tend to their wounded was particularly touchy, especially in light of lawsuits some players have brought against their former employers. Beyond that, former Oakland Raiders team physician Robert Huizenga had written a book claiming widespread abuses, instances where team doctors risked their patients' health in the name of winning football games.

"This is not an isolated incident," Huizenga told *Sports*

photo by Vernon Biever

Favre can always draw a crowd in Green Bay, but the mob scene at
his post-treatment press conference was almost unprecedented.

Illustrated after Favre came forward with his painkiller revelation. "We want people to play hurt, and when someone doesn't play hurt, he's no longer our hero. We need a system where a physician, without fear of losing his job, can say to an athlete, 'The injury is not healed. You cannot play.'"

So the matter of how NFL teams handle their injured personnel seemed to be hanging over the Favre case, although from the beginning, no one claimed that Packers team doctor John Gray had acted unprofessionally in any way whatsoever.

Meanwhile, on the personal side, perhaps the most intriguing question of all that could only be answered by No. 4 himself was this: Would the formerly brash, bold, take-no-prisoners Brett Favre — Green Bay's hell-bent, head-knockin' gunslinger — return meek, chastened, humbled or apologetic after his ordeal?

Several people close to Favre already knew his state of mind and guessed just what the public was going to hear.

Packers center Frank Winters, one of Brett's closest friends on the team, actually had visited Favre during his six-week stay at the Menninger Clinic in Topeka, Kansas. Winters lives in suburban Kansas City and made the hour drive west to check on his buddy's progress about halfway through treatment.

"I really wasn't sure what to expect," Winters said, "but I know Brett, and he's as tough as it gets. You know that being in a facility like that is going to be hard, because it's serious business, but if you could pick one guy to fight through a thing like that, Brett's the guy."

And when Winters got to Topeka? Were there tears, hugs, heart-to-heart talks about the much-publicized seizure Favre had suffered prior to entering the clinic? Did the two men talk about the larger issues of life?

"Actually, we went out and played golf," Winters said. "Just like before. As far as I could tell, he was the same old Brett. He just wanted to get through it and get home. I knew he'd come out rarin' to go."

Former Packers quarterback Lynn Dickey, the man who in 1982 led Green Bay to its last pre-Favre appearance in the play-offs — and himself a recovered painkiller addict — had watched Brett up close for a couple of seasons while doing a Wisconsin-area radio show.

Dickey thought he knew exactly what would happen at Favre's coming-out meeting with the media. "If Brett were in charge of the thing," Dickey said, "this would be the shortest press conference in history. He'd just walk out there, grin at everybody and say, 'Hey, guys, I screwed up. I went and got it fixed. Now let's get our asses out there and play some football.' Big smile. End of press conference. That's Brett.

"They won't let him do it exactly like that, obviously, but anybody who's waiting for this kid to come in there hanging his head just doesn't know him."

Favre's daddy, Irvin, suspected the same thing. Even as he waited at home in Mississippi during his son's rehabilitation, Irvin remained steadfast.

"The harder you knock Brett down, the quicker and

tougher he gets back up," the elder Favre said. "He's always been that way on the field, and this won't be any different. I know these pills were bad, and he had to get the treatment, but my boy isn't going get licked by anything like this. He'll be just fine. You'll see. He'll get well and get back to playing football."

Packers office personnel, meanwhile, got to see the post-rehab Favre a couple of weeks before anyone else. The team didn't want Brett talking to any reporters until a formal press gathering could be convened, and that wasn't going to happen without Holmgren around. Since the coach was on vacation until July 14, the team welcomed Favre back on the premises the first week of the month, but a gag rule was imposed.

No interviews, formal or otherwise. For a good ol' boy like Brett Favre, who has bona fide pals in the press corps and normally is as forthcoming as any star athlete, that decision must have been akin to telling Pavarotti not to sing.

But there were hints. Packer executives told friends that Brett was back and seemed every bit like the same character they knew and loved. He was roaming the premises, telling stories, butting into conversations, hopping on people's desks, joking with secretaries — in short, acting very much as though he'd never been anywhere except on a bass-fishing vacation in Mississippi.

And sure enough, once the momentous press conference got started, it turned out that Brett was still Brett. Except better.

The thing started with the proper somber tones, as

Holmgren – who orchestrated the whole deal and deflected any questions he deemed "too personal" — lectured the assembled multitude about team medical guidelines (which were given a clean bill by the NFL) and Favre's rights under the league's patient confidentiality rules.

At the coach's shoulder, the man of the hour sat quietly, trying to look serious and thoughtful, while Holmgren was laying down his laws. Still, it didn't take long for the real Brett Favre to take charge.

No, he never went so far as to blow off his bout with Vicodin as something you'd treat like a common cold. Favre often referred to feeling badly about hurting his family, his friends and his teammates by letting this painkiller intrude into his life. But Brett also made it crystal clear that he considered his problem in the past tense, and that it was time to be gettin' on with the future. And that meant winning football games.

Responding to a question about whether he expected a hostile reaction from fans in other cities, Favre laughed out loud. "I never really got a great response from opposing fans, anyway," he said. "But I don't expect it to be any better this year. I expect pill bottles will be thrown at me. Whiskey bottles. Beer bottles. But that's OK. That's what makes this game great, to go into another place and beat teams in a hostile environment."

And just as Lynn Dickey had forecast, Favre insisted that the trouble was over.

"This is behind me," he said. "I just let it get out of hand last year. Thankfully, I caught it before it got bad.

"Injuries did bring me into contact with pain medication. Eventually, it became a problem. More injuries would pile up. All of a sudden, I just started taking them, and it was a snowball effect. It was something I just couldn't control.

"It doesn't make you a bad person to be addicted to anything. That you can't control. I used to think alcoholics were bums in the street. I used to think that a drug addict was a bum, a loser. It's totally the opposite. It's OK to come forward. Sometimes, people won't understand, but it's for yourself. It's not for the people out there, it's for yourself and your family."

Likewise, Irvin Favre was correct in his judgment that Brett would equate his battle to shake Vicodin with wars on the football field. And that Brett would be more than ready to once again start firing passes at NFL defenses.

"Everyone I talked to is talking Super Bowl," Favre said, presumably referring to his teammates rather than doctors, counselors or even the media. "Last year at this time, no one was. We were hoping to get into the playoffs.

"All the guys are in the best shape I've ever seen them in. I'm not saying it took me going into rehab, but something happened. I feel very good about this year. Mentally, I'm ready to play. That's scary. Because if I can play as well as I did last year the way I was...I'm not saying I can throw 50 touchdown passes, but I feel the best I ever have."

And certainly Favre looked the part. Perhaps bright-eyed and bushy-tailed is a hoary old cliche, but it seemed to fit. In addition to his clear gaze and peaceful countenance, Favre also turned up lean and hard 15 pounds lighter than the puffy-faced fellow who had last spoken to the media on the occasion of his I-have-sinned announcement.

By the standards of your average Packers fan, the press conference seemed just this side of a godsend. Brett was back, he was healthy, he was joking, he was committed to football and apparently driven more than ever to the task of taking Green Bay to the Super Bowl.

Brother, did that show ever play well in the Dairy State. After all, this wasn't a third-string tight end fighting a personal problem, it was Brett Favre, the Packers' golden gun who had thrown 71 touchdown passes and only 17 interceptions over the past two seasons — the second-best two-year TD to pickoff ratio in NFL history. In 1995 alone, Favre unloaded 38 TD throws (the league's third-highest total ever) and racked up 4,413 yards. Not to mention leading the Packers to the NFC Central Division championship, their first since 1972, and two resounding playoff victories.

Television commentators gushed. Radio and TV microphones seemed to find just about every man, woman and child on the streets of Green Bay. Across the state, newspaper headlines blared the good news.

"Fresh Start for Favre," gushed the *Green Bay Press-Gazette* in screaming bold type. Down in Milwaukee, the *Journal Sentinel* led Page 1 of the paper with a color photo from the press conference and a headline which said: "Favre Vows He's Overcome Past."

Of course, a lot of ticklish questions either went

unanswered — matters of where the Vicodin came from and how much Favre was taking were off-limits — and a few more caused some health-care professionals to fret out loud.

For one thing, experts on addiction chimed in from all over the landscape. Most expressed concern over several things: Favre's apparent dismissal of the seizure, which he claimed doctors assured him was never life-threatening; his certainty that the addiction was over ("Some part of your body will always crave a drug," one Green Bay-area treatment counselor warned…); his light-hearted approach to post-rehab therapy — he suggested everybody could use it once in awhile — and most of all, Brett's assertion that alcohol did not contribute to the problem and would not cause him any particular grief in the future.

The drinking question presumably will stay on hold for at least two years, since Favre's agreement with the league calls for random drug testing that includes alcohol. "Mark (Chmura) and Frank and I will just have to have Cokes and pizza after games," Favre said.

But the notion left dangling was that the day after his mandated clean period expires, Brett feels he'll be free and safe to quaff a beer or two with his pals.

Consider this rebuttal, an oft-repeated story by respected California drug and alcohol counselor Joe Garcia: "Substances that alter your mind might look different and taste different, but an addict is an addict. It lasts a lifetime. And the fastest way back to your drug of choice (Vicodin in Favre's case) is through another drug.

"Believe me, I know the story. I was hooked on hard

drugs and got off. Stayed off for years. Then one day I was feeling really good and relaxed and I saw this cold, delicious bottle of Lowenbrau beer. It looked wonderful, and I'm thinking there's no way one great bottle of beer can hurt me.

"Less than 24 hours later, I was driving all over, looking for old drug connections, and that same day I spiked some heroin in my arm. I can tell you all about one cold beer."

You'll find Lynn Dickey on the opposite side of the same argument. Dickey says he got hooked on painkillers — not once, but twice — from the battering he took as a pro quarterback, but quit the drugs on his own and has suffered no relapses from alcohol or anything else.

"There's no question I went through the same thing as Brett," Dickey said. "The first time was when I broke my hip. They gave me shots for the pain, because there was nerve damage and it really, really hurt. It seemed to go on and on and on.

"I got dependent on the shots, and then I realized that after the pain finally went away, I still wanted my shots. The docs would ask me, 'Does it hurt?' and I'm thinking: Well, no, not anymore. But I'd say, 'Yeah, I need a shot.'

"Then when I broke my leg, I got hooked on a combination of sleeping pills and painkillers. I knew exactly what was going on, because I kept taking them after the leg stopped hurting. I'd always know when it was 2 o'clock, because "Guiding Light" came on TV and I knew it was time for a pill and my little afternoon buzz.

"I might have kept taking the pills, too, except that

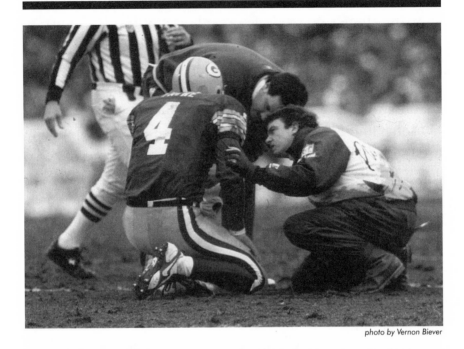

There's no question how Favre's addiction to painkillers grew so acute:
He took a physical pounding in his first four seasons as a starter.

they just ran out and I didn't have the guts to ask for any more. So I just bit the bullet and quit. I was up three straight nights doing crossword puzzles, but then it was over.

"I'm not worried about Brett at all. Not one bit."

There surely are similarities between the cases of Dickey and Favre, although Dickey never made his problem public nor sought any kind of treatment. This may be the first anyone in the Packer family has heard of Lynn's flirtation with narcotic painkillers.

Like Dickey, Favre stopped taking the Vicodin on his own — cold turkey, and well before he entered the treatment center. Perhaps he was frightened by the seizure (which more likely was caused by Demerol he received after ankle surgery), or he was alarmed at the number of pills he needed to feel good. Certainly the insistence of then-fiancé, now-wife Deanna Tynes had some influence on Brett's decision to cleanse his system. Or maybe he was just feeling lousy.

Whatever the reasons that Favre chose to consult team and NFL doctors about the problem and agree to their prescribed treatment, the quarterback isn't changing his mind about the fact that the trouble is over.

When he was asked at the now-famous July 17 press conference if he worried about a relapse, Favre responded, "Believe it or not, no. And that kind of scared the people at the treatment center who were working on me. They said you've got to think about it every day. Well, I'm not everybody.

"You know, I've always been that way. Mike will tell me something, and I'd probably do the opposite. My parents would tell me something, and I'd do totally the opposite. You know I'm going to beat this thing. I'm going to the Super Bowl. All I can tell people is if they don't believe me, just bet against me."

Brett anticipated one of the most obvious reactions to his drug treatment. No matter how much he'd like it to go away, no matter how certain he might be that the Vicodin is just an unpleasant piece of history, the guy realizes that his face is on dozens of magazine covers and every series of downs from now on will be scrutinized in a different light.

"Just to reassure you guys," he said, "there will be times this year (1996) when there will be interceptions and games when I could have played better. I don't want to be sitting here again having to answer questions like, 'Is it caused because you didn't take painkillers? Or did you take them again?'

"That's behind me. That's what's going to be tough. If we can all forget about this. Because I have."

Brett is no dummy, however, so he knows the memory of his problem will linger, and he won't be allowed to ignore it completely.

That's particularly true because the man has endured a string of horrendous injuries dating back to his car accident in college, yet still entered the 1996 season with the longest string of consecutive starts (68) of any quarterback in the NFL. Skeptics wonder what will happen when he wrenches a shoulder or twists a knee in the future.

Favre's list of injuries is staggering: He had endured

five operations in six years. Even as recently as 1995, Brett had surgery for a herniated muscle in his right side, suffered from a lingering turf toe problem and badly sprained the right ankle on which he must plant to throw — the problem that led eventually to more post-season surgery and the hospital stay during which he endured the frightening seizure that caused his seven-year daughter to ask if her father was going to die.

Addressing one obvious concern for the media, Holmgren claimed his star now will be treated only with non-addictive pain medication and, further, that the drugs that hooked him really didn't have anything to do with keeping him on the football field.

As an example, Holmgren cited a terribly sprained ankle that Favre suffered at Minnesota midway through the '95 season. The injury was so painful that, for once, even tough-guy Favre couldn't get back on the field and the Packers blew a very winnable game because backup QB Ty Detmer also got hurt and No. 3 guy T.J. Rubley threw an incredibly ill-advised interception in the final minute of play.

Even though that defeat at Minnesota put the Packers in a precarious state in the Central Division race, it didn't seem that there was any way Favre could play the following week against the Bears, but he got the ankle taped so heavily that it was almost a walking cast. Brett limped around on the injured wheel and gutted his way through every offensive play.

"There was no medication administered that day,"

Holmgren said. "His ankle was wrapped up tight, his ankle was stiff, he got through it. It's not like he took a bunch of pills so he could play."

That game will live forever in Packer lore: Favre didn't practice all week and admitted afterward that he had no idea what to expect. "Before the game, me and several players were talking, saying this was the most nervous we had been in years, probably dating back to college," Favre said. "I'd been hurt all week and didn't know if I was going to come back. It was really a big game all around."

Big?

It was huge. Favre completed an almost unbelievable 25 of 33 passes for 336 yards and five touchdowns, without an interception, as the Packers rallied in the fourth quarter to win 35-28 — setting the course for their eventual division title.

In light of the later Vicodin revelations, it was no surprise that Holmgren picked that particular performance to back up his assertion that the painkillers — however dangerous they became in Brett's personal life — really had no effect on his week-to-week ability to play football.

Actually, questions about what Brett had been putting in his system might have been inevitable, even if he'd never entered a treatment program.

Some of the naysayers who wonder what kept Favre upright through so many frightful injuries perhaps took some of Brett's own shoot-from-the-lip comments too seriously over the years. Prior to the duel with Vicodin, Favre always seemed to be joking about pain shots or laughing about living a wild, beer-swilling existence. His family and friends, though, all insist that the image far outstripped reality — particularly in recent years.

"I wouldn't even call Brett a party guy in the past year or two," Winters said. "All of us calmed down a lot, with family obligations and so forth. Brett had the responsibility of being a team leader, and Brittany (his daughter) to take care of. He was home a lot more than he was out anywhere, believe me."

So for now, that's where the issue stands. As Favre says, if you doubt, bet against him.

In just about every challenge Brett Favre has faced up to now, that hasn't been a very good idea. And if the painkiller episode made one thing perfectly clear, it was that Favre remains the stubborn, independent, tough-minded fighter he's been since childhood.

As a matter of fact, that's the story of his life.

CHAPTER TWO:
GOOD BOY, BAD BOY

What a lovefest it was.

On March 25, 1996, all Milwaukee was abuzz over a simple old luncheon — cold chicken Kiev and so forth — that had turned into a major-league event. The occasion was the naming of Wisconsin's Sportsperson of the Year, and the recipient was none other than every cheesehead's hero, Brett Favre.

Actually, the regular program for this annual affair called for some chit-chat by officials from the local sports authority, presentation of certificates to the state's top male and female high school athletes and, finally, introduction of the star attraction. Followed, of course, by remarks and a question-and-answer session with the audience.

Normally, this noontime gathering — one hour time limit, so all the suit-and-tie types could be back at work downtown just after 1 p.m. — would draw maybe a couple hundred folks. A few niceties, appropriate applause, and then everybody getting on about their regular Thursday afternoon business.

But there was nothing normal about the gala that was coming together this particular year. Not with Favre making an appearance. Nope. In Milwaukee, this was just a step short of a papal visit.

First off, the site had to be changed when event organizers realized that seats were being snapped up like tickets to a Packer playoff game. Just for a ho-hum meal and the chance to hear Brett Favre say thanks, more or less, reservations soared past the 1,000 mark. And the luncheon had to be moved to the spacious Bradley Center just to accommodate the crowd.

And sure enough, the place was buzzed a half-hour before noon. No offense to the worthy prep athletes being honored, but the drawing card was Favre, who was to be ushered to the head table — with great fanfare — after everyone was seated.

Brett even dressed up for the occasion, at least by Brett's own sartorial standards. The good people of Milwaukee should have been proud that their favorite quarterback turned up wearing a sport coat instead of his everyday get-up — T-shirt, shorts and sandals. He didn't go quite so far as putting on a tie, but hey, No. 4 would almost need an invitation to the White House for that sort of formality.

Lee Remmel, the Packers longtime public relations director and himself a member of the Wisconsin Sports Hall of Fame, sought out Favre in the corner office where he'd been sequestered just before lunch. Besides wanting to check in and say hello, Remmel couldn't resist a chance to jibe with one of his all-time favorite players.

These two – young millionaire quarterback and gray-haired, overworked PR executive – truly enjoy needling one another. Remmel insists on calling Favre by his middle name, Lorenzo, and Brett returns serve, relentlessly, by imitating Remmel's deep voice to make hilarious remarks.

"Well, now, Lorenzo, I almost didn't recognize you," Remmel said. "I wasn't scanning the crowd for a sport coat. You're looking especially dapper."

Favre was grinning and promptly dropped into his Lee voice. "But you'll notice," he replied, "that I've accented my coat with this attractive gravy stain."

And so the mood of the luncheon was set.

For the public, it went off even better than imagined. Lauded by one speaker after another, Favre watched a tape of himself specially prepared by NFL Films — combination touchdown passes and Brett singing country songs on the sidelines during the magic 1995 season — and then was introduced by Packer general manager Ron Wolf.

That was on honor in itself. Wolf is a football workaholic who has acceptable, but hardly comfortable social skills and rarely ventures out onto the ham-and-yam circuit. Ron would rather be in seclusion scouting college players on tape than making speeches for businessmen at lunchtime.

But Wolf rose to the occasion and did a wonderful job, recalling how he first came to notice Favre prior to the 1991 draft while bird-dogging talent as personnel director for the New York Jets. Wolf's tale of his trip to Hattiesburg,

Mississippi, was a good one, and Favre chuckled all the way through it.

Then finally, the man of the hour himself was officially introduced and stepped to the microphone. Brett Favre, country boy who once had an overpowering fear of speaking in public, wasted no time winning over the audience. Not only that, he worked the room like a pro.

Oh, Favre went through the obligatory thank-yous, but he also got the crowd laughing by turning to ask Wolf — after all those kind words — if, gee, couldn't we work out a bigger contract right on the spot.

The most amazing thing about Favre's performance that day was that he seemed so polished, as though he'd been the NFL's most valuable player a half-dozen times and had a stock speech in hand. Brett's timing with funny lines would have done justice to the best stand-up comedians. His facial expressions changed exactly on cue, and he somehow came off both cocky and humble.

It was a five-star show, and when questions came from the audience, Favre handled them the way he runs the Packer offense — first option, second option, look down the middle, pick the right receiver, move the chains, pump his fists.

And the audience lapped it up.

When a questioner wanted to know the toughest road stadiums in the league, Brett thought a minute and said, "Well, I've got to say Dallas, don't I?"

Cue the laughter...

"And Kansas City, which is really loud, so it's hard to

hear and change things at the line. I guess it would be Dallas and Kansas City."

The questions moved on to other areas, Favre did his shtick and everybody howled. And then a fellow way in back, who obviously hadn't heard the earlier give-and-take — maybe he'd been in the bathroom — hollered out the very same question Brett already had answered about the toughest stadiums in the league.

The instant this guy finished his question, everybody in the building knew what was going on. Some snickered, a couple frowned, a few more looked around to see where the inquiry was coming from. It was like, hey, let's not be bothering our superstar with silly repeat questions, pal.

But Favre played it like a pro. He paused one beat, two beats, three...letting the room titter awhile...and then screwed up his face in deep concentration.

"Let me think about that one," he said, finally, drawing another laugh. "You know, I'd say — heck, that's a tough one — I'd say Dallas and Kansas City."

And naturally, the room went nuts. Brett and the faithful were having great kicks together, a big old happy party. It was a boffo performance.

At last, Favre wrapped up with more thanks and words of appreciation, and lunch was history. Thundering applause. The entire affair was a howling success, and no doubt everyone filed back out into the chilly spring rain just hopelessly in love with Brett Favre.

Accepting congratulations later, Favre could only smile and shake his head considering how smooth he'd been.

"Maybe I'm getting better because I had a big year and I've spent the winter receiving awards," he said. "I've had a lot more practice giving speeches than I'm used to."

But even Favre knew that wasn't explanation enough.

"It's weird," he said, "but when I was a kid in grade school, I couldn't even stand up in front of a class to give a book report. That kind of thing would scare me to death.

"You know, my dad was a football coach all that time I was growing up, and I'd go to these banquets and awards things where he was a speaker, and I'd hear him say all the right stuff and make people laugh. Or be serious. Or whatever he wanted. I just couldn't imagine how he could do that. I asked him about it one time and he told me, 'All I do is think about gettin' up there and having fun. It's not like a real speech, it's just talking to your friends. If you have fun, they'll have fun and everything works out.' "

Favre said he thought about his dad's philosophy on public speaking a bit and when the time came — in college, in pro football — where he had to meet the media and public himself, he just decided daddy knows best. Go with the flow.

"It's easy for me now and I really do like it," Brett said. "I get up thinking I'm going to have myself a good old time, and pretty soon the audience is doing the same thing. I just go be myself and it works out just fine."

And it *had* come off perfectly in Milwaukee. On the two-hour drive back up to Green Bay after lunch, Lee Remmel remarked how slick, how professional, how mature Favre had become at handling his fame.

"He's come to understand both sides of his job, the football and the public," Remmel said. "Today he just showed up and knocked out the crowd at that lunch, and this afternoon it'll be back to business."

In fact, that's exactly how the schedule was supposed to work out. Favre, Wolf, Brett's agent Bus Cook and another passenger were booked for a private jet flight out of Milwaukee. They were scheduled to flee the Bradley Center before the last dish was cleared away. Quick limo ride to the airport, and zoom, off to Green Bay. Favre had a meeting with coach Mike Holmgren set for that afternoon, a let's-get-started session to open a weekend mini-camp that began the next day.

Imagine Remmel's surprise when he arrived at Lambeau Field around 3:30 and found the 6-foot-5 Holmgren looming the hallway with a serious scowl on his face. "Did you guys just get back from Milwaukee?" Holmgren said. Remmel barely had time to nod yes when Holmgren shot back, "Where's Brett? We have a meeting and he's late. Very late."

Needless to say, Remmel had no idea of Favre's whereabouts. The last anyone had seen of Favre, he was in Wolf's care and they were rushing to the airport in Milwaukee.

"He was with Ron?" Holmgren asked. Another nod. And then the coach stalked off, banging open a door on his way upstairs. Not a happy man.

Remmel was completely puzzled by the entire affair, but what the heck, the general manager had Favre in tow, so everybody's backside ought to be covered. There were other public relations duties on tap, so Lee went back to work and forgot about the missing quarterback.

Now flash forward to the next day. Favre had agreed to do an interview in a conference room adjacent to Remmel's office. Brett showed up pretty much right on time, still wearing some of his workout clothes from that afternoon's practice.

The question just begged to be asked: Say, Brett, what happened to you yesterday? Did you get in trouble with Mike? He seemed pretty upset.

And in a heartbeat, the grown-up Brett Favre who handled a thousand admirers with incredible ease the previous day changed into his other personality. He was Huck Finn again.

"Well, yeah, I was late and Mike was kinda mad," Brett said with a sheepish kind of grin. "We were supposed to go right to the airport, you know, and fly up to Green Bay, then drive right to the stadium.

"But there was a delay in Milwaukee. I don't know, they had to file flight plans or something, and load baggage, some stuff like that. So we got off late. And then we got to Green Bay, Bus was with me and I had to drop him off. Now normally I would have come right to the stadium — that was the plan — but like I said, Bus was there and...

"Truthfully? From the time I finished my speech at the lunch, all the way to the plane and during the flight, I mean, I had to go to the bathroom real bad. There just didn't seem like a place to stop. So when we got back, I still

Brett Favre can be deadly serious about preparing for a football game, or
sometimes just a laid-back country boy having a good old time.

had to go and I had Bus with me so I went home first. I had to get to the bathroom *really* badly. And then I came to the stadium and found Mike, and..."

Wait a minute, Brett. You were late for a meeting with the head coach because you drove to your house to use the toilet? Something wrong with the facilities at Lambeau Field?

"Uh, no, but see, we were already late, and if I'd come to the stadium first, then..."

Never mind, son.

Holmgren's take on his quarterback's tardiness: "Sometimes Brett's excuses are so long and so complicated that, no matter how you try to follow what he's saying, he just keeps going until you get lost. He really can be a little kid at times like that. It's like having a seven-year old. He knows if he just keeps talking, he'll wear you out."

And there, in a nutshell, you find both sides of Brett Favre. Which, of course, is why he's so lovable. Among other things.

There's really still the barefoot boy getting in trouble and making excuses lurking inside this strapping lad, but Brett also has grown into a mature man of the world. He's a leader and he knows it. He has responsibilities and when they're important enough, he'll meet them, no matter what. He certainly proved that point in the painkiller treatment episode — not so much by admitting he needed professional help and getting it, but by stepping to the podium at a grim press conference to tell the world of his problems.

"I've had other players tell me they never could have done that press conference," Favre said. "I could have done it all privately, keep it quiet, gotten treatment and held everything within the family. But that wouldn't have helped other people with the same problems. It just wasn't the right thing to do."

Favre clearly can be brave beyond the call of duty. He's what men, when they're describing each other, refer to as a stand-up guy. Big time.

Yet this is the same Brett Favre who plays practical jokes on anybody foolish enough to let his guard down, who chuckles in the huddle and sings on the sidelines, who gets involved in silly pranks and then tries to talk his way out of the doghouse like a kid faced with a trip to the principal's office.

Listen to Mark McHale, the Southern Mississippi assistant coach who first spotted Favre playing at Hancock North Central High School and wound up — by hook and crook — convincing the rest of the Southern Miss coaching staff to offer Brett a scholarship.

"Best way I can describe this boy," McHale said, "is that he's like your little ol' cocker spaniel. He'll make a mess or knock over the furniture, you know, but he's gonna make you love him anyhow. Somehow, that spaniel's gonna get you to pat him on the head no matter what he does. That's Brett."

Favre's two closest pals on the Packers are center Frank Winters and tight end Mark Chmura. "The three amigos," moaned Holmgren. "Whenever something funny's going on, something's not right, they're the automatic suspects. And most of the time, they're guilty.

"I finally figured out how to deal with them. When trouble comes, I call 'em in to my office, but I always tell them, 'Look, if somebody tells me up front what happened, then it'll be OK. Just don't string me along.'

"Then I talk to each of them, and they never have time to get their stories straight with each other, and somebody screws it up, and I've got 'em.'"

Winters admits he's constantly amazed by Favre's cheekiness in the tightly controlled atmosphere of a pro football operation. "Brett just wanders around the place like he owns it," Winters said. "Listen, it isn't just secretaries or equipment guys he talks to. Brett will walk right into Bob Harlan's office. The president. Just walk right in. Same thing with Mike's office. Brett just walks in, like it's no big deal. Ask any other NFL player about doing something like that and they can't believe it. The rest of us would die before we'd go someplace without an appointment.

"Brett, it doesn't mean a thing to him. And somehow, no matter what he does, nobody can stay mad at him."

Ah, yes. The cocker spaniel.

Here's the take from Clark Henegan, a college pal of Favre's who moved to Green Bay to help manage his friend's day-to-day chores: "He's the biggest prankster there is. If you're not careful, he'll pull your pants down on the tee box. Trust me."

In fact, Favre did exactly that to Steve Mariucci, his quarterback coach and confidant until Mariucci left for the head coaching job at California after the 1995 season.

"The worst part was they had it on film," Mariucci said. "That's just how he is. He's the funniest human being I've ever been around. To be witty, you have to be intelligent, and he's very witty. Not that I ever want him to do *that* again."

Mariucci, though, always has been quick to point out that Favre's hijinks don't interfere with the business of football. And that the guy he helped mold into the league's MVP understands when it's time to play and time to work.

"We have a great mutual respect," Mariucci said during an interview in early 1996, and when I say, 'we,' I mean all the quarterbacks. "It's a constant Barnum and Bailey, but when it's time to go, we go. We get after it and there's no fooling around.

"Brett's image used to be the...well, you know. Now his image and persona is that he's an intelligent quarterback. Heads-up. Gutsy. He's playing the position very well and very smart. He's playing a little bit beyond the scheme of our system at times with his improvising and making good things happen. (But) he's keeping the negatives to a minimum."

Everyone involved with the Packers organization agrees that despite all the clowning around and even the scary bout with painkillers, Favre is every inch a leader — the man who will shoulder the load when those big chips are down.

"He's definitely grown up year by year," Holmgren said. "You don't just walk into the NFL and know how to handle every situation. And he didn't. There were times...aw, that's

Favre once had the reputation of a guy who wasn't eager to keep himself in shape, but that image has changed.

another story. But the point is that Brett knows he's our guy, the guy his teammates look to for leadership.

"His style isn't ever going to be one of the stone-faced, take-charge boss who makes everybody afraid of him. He's having too much fun living his life and playing football for that. But that doesn't mean he hasn't developed into a bona fide leader in this league."

Chmura thinks the turning point in Favre's emergence as more than just a raw talent who could gun the football came after all-pro receiver Sterling Sharpe was forced to retire with a serious neck injury. Chmura recalls a 1994 game in Milwaukee against Atlanta, the Packers' first without Sharpe, as the true start of The Favre Era.

"The first couple years playing here," Chmura said, "Sterling was the guy and Brett wasn't and I think that bothered Brett at times. That (Atlanta game) was the first time where Brett had a bunch of no-names in the huddle and took the ball right down the field and won a big game that put us in the playoffs.

"I think that's when he really matured and when this team matured. I think that's what he wanted from the start (to be the team leader). But the whole Sterling thing kind of hindered him and I think Brett wanted that role, and he's done a great job with it. He's such a competitive guy personally and I know everybody on this team wouldn't want anybody else but Brett back there."

Favre seems to understand both sides of his image, and frankly, he likes 'em both. He's also quite aware of the strides he's made as a quarterback — in maturity, decision-making and, of course, the leadership job.

"I've come so far," Favre said. "I look back and laugh. I think every quarterback can tell you that."

At the time he made that statement, Favre happened to be discussing a couple of plays he executed in a win over Tampa Bay. Each time, he'd checked off the called play after reading the Bucs defense.

"The thing about it was how calm I did it," Favre said. "Just kind of looked out there and checked. My first couple years, I would be doing all this stuff and the play kind of was like that.

"I've learned so much over the years. You have to live and learn. You have to go through your mistakes. This offense is so hard. It's even hard to explain how hard it is. There are so many things that can happen on one play, and you have so many plays."

No matter how much of a good ol' boy image Favre has projected, particularly when he and his buddies decide it's time for a fall-down laugh, nobody ever has questioned Brett's work ethic.

A stranger to the weight room during his college career, Favre has come to realize that he has to work like a demon to keep his body intact for NFL wars. Now he's something of a fitness fanatic, a weight-room regular even on the Packers' off days.

"Everybody assumes that the first thing that struck me about Brett was that great arm, the natural talent," said Jeff Bower, who was Favre's offensive coordinator at Southern Mississippi and is now that school's head coach. "Sure, the gun was there and he could do some pretty amazing things.

"But what I remember most was how much Brett wanted to be a good player, and how hard he'd work at it. I think some people figured, especially when he was back at Southern Miss, that Brett was just this kid from a little high school who came in with a super arm and had success just throwing the ball as hard as he could.

"Hey, he learned things so fast it was amazing. I'll never forget coming in to work on Mondays — the staff hadn't even met yet to start putting in a game plan for the next week — and Brett would be there waiting for us, saying, 'OK, what have we got. What are we gonna do with this team?'

"I think at times he developed so fast that it actually hurt our football team. We started out with a pretty simple passing game, but we had to keep adding things all the time just to keep Brett challenged, to keep him interested. It might have worked out that when we added stuff that he caught on right away, but some of it was too much for the other guys. We probably had breakdowns and some big mistakes that cost us because Brett could do so many things, we got carried away.

"The whole point, though, is that this guy was an unbelievably fast learner, and he wanted it. I can't tell you how much he wanted it, and you can see watching him improve game by game, year by year at Green Bay that he's still the same way. He demands a lot of himself because he's driven to succeed, and for Brett Favre, succeeding isn't completions or touchdowns or any of that stuff.

"Brett is all about winning games, and he'll work all

day and all night figuring out how to win. So when I think back to our days with Brett, I'll always think of Monday mornings. He was rarin' to go."

In that area, pure competitiveness coupled with natural skills at the quarterback position, Favre now is often compared with San Francisco's Steve Young, a proven star running the same "West Coast" offense. Both are gut-tough gamers who will chew through a wooden fence to beat you — and each was tutored by Holmgren, who was offensive coordinator for the 49ers when Young emerged as the successor to Joe Montana.

"They're completely different individuals off the field," Holmgren said of Young and Favre, but they're a lot alike when the ball is snapped. You don't want to get in these guys' way. Each of them took some time grasping the offense — like Brett says, it's tough — and they hated screwing something up. But they're the kinds of guys who will just keep working like crazy to get it right."

Favre relished the comparisons with Young so much that he was practically jumping out of his skin with excitement when the Packers finally were matched up against the mighty 49ers in the 1995 playoffs.

For one thing, Favre remembered studying Young in previous seasons, watching for clues to operating this complicated offense. At the Pro Bowl one year, Brett actually decided to pick Young's brain about some particular nuances.

"It's kind of like Chinese arithmetic," Favre said. "You can sit there and look at it all day and you're like, why do you do this? Why do you do that? Why is it called this? That's kind of what I was talking to (Young) about."

Young's response? "He was like, 'Young punk'," Brett said. "He could care less what I was saying." And then Favre laughed. He wants to make sure everyone knows he was kidding, that he thinks Young is the best quarterback in football. Remember, with Brett, sometimes you can't tell just when he's being serious and when he's pulling your leg.

Favre's admiration for Young and the 49ers was genuine, though, which is why Brett was so thrilled with his performance in the Packers' 27-17 victory at San Francisco. Favre was 21 of 28 for 299 yards with two touchdowns and no interceptions against one of the game's best defenses.

Here's another little insight toward how much Favre has matured. Since the Packers and 49ers run almost identical offenses, Holmgren changed his team's entire system of audibles for that game.

"A couple of years ago, I wouldn't have done that," Holmgren said. He couldn't have been sure Favre would adjust without the whole thing falling apart around him. By playoff time 1995, the coach had no doubt at all.

Favre was properly respectful while talking to the media after that triumph at Candlestick Park, careful not to say anything even remotely critical of the 49ers — a team Holmgren coached and which both men admire.

But Brett did let a little of his playful nature show through. As usual, he couldn't help himself. "Who knows?" he said. "Maybe this year, somebody will try to pick my brain."

Anyone who does would find it full of good cheer and honest-to-God enjoyment at playing the game of football. They'll also discover an awful lot of Xs and Os.

"People are always going to call Brett a country boy," his father Irvin said, "and that's fine, because that's what he is. But I hope they don't say country and mean dumb, 'cause that'd be a big mistake. The boy is very, very bright."

It's just that sometimes, he has to pull down somebody's pants to prove it.

CHAPTER THREE:
WAY DOWN YONDER

To know Brett Favre, you have to go to Rotten Bayou. There really is such a place, though tourists aren't likely to stumble across it by accident. In fact, plenty of people — mostly Packer fans on pilgrimages from Wisconsin — have bumped across the back roads of southern Mississippi actually *looking* for Rotten Bayou and still gotten lost.

Don't do it at night, Yankee, or the gators'll git ya.

Now that he's grown up and become a man in his mid-20s, not to mention a multimillionaire and the hottest young quarterback in the National Football League, Favre's upbringing on the banks of Rotten Bayou has become a subject of curiosity for fans and tidbit-hungry members of the media.

Did the boy go to school barefoot, or what? Did the Favre family have indoor plumbing, or stand in line to use the outhouse?

Green Bay center Frank Winters, originally a New Jersey

photo by Vernon Biever

kid who has become one of Favre's closest friends, laughed when asked to describe his pal's boyhood home. "It's a nice place, honestly," he said. "I'm sure it was a great place to grow up. But I've got to tell you, it's right at the end of civilization. When Mark (Chmura) and I went out there to visit, we kind of stood looking into the bayou behind their house and went, 'Man, this is like the movie *Deliverance*.' "

Chmura echoed Winters' sentiments. "It's an eye-opening experience," Chmura said. "It's a different world. Shoot, where Brett's from, there are alligators swimming 25 yards from the house — and he wants to go swimming in there. It's an experience. If you saw it, water moccasins and stuff, and they're all swimming right there. Frank and I looked at Brett like he was nuts."

Despite being just a few minutes off the interstate, the Favres do live in what could only be described as a slice of wilderness. There really are gators in the bayou — Brett lost one of his dogs to one, or at least that's what the family assumed when the labrador disappeared — and snakes are everywhere.

"We've had to fish a couple of cottonmouths out of the swimming pool," Bonita Favre said. "That'll get your attention first thing in the morning. Snakes really aren't my best friends. I don't want much to do with them."

Which isn't necessarily true for her husband.

Irvin tells a story about sitting in the party room, a separate structure from their main house, and chatting on the phone one day with Brett's agent, Bus Cook, up in Hattiesburg. "I told him, 'Wait a minute, Bus, there's a big ol' snake over there by the door,' " Irvin said. "And Bus said, 'You mean, inside?' I told him yeah, and he wanted to know what I was gonna do about it, like maybe I was going to grab a shotgun or something. I just said, 'Nothing. He ain't bothering anybody.' I think Bus thought I must be crazy."

Back to the geography: How would a visitor, assuming he's willing to step carefully around the wildlife, go about finding Rotten Bayou?

Listen to Al Jones, who became a buddy of Brett's at the University of Southern Mississippi and now makes a living writing about hunting and fishing for the *Sun Herald* newspaper down in the Gulfport-Biloxi area: "Well now, a tourist coming up the interstate from New Orleans ain't goin' to have an easy time, because the exit to Kiln (the hamlet officially listed as Favre's hometown) doesn't really take you to the Favres' house."

In fact, that turnoff for highways 43 and 603 will run you through Kiln — past the sign for Beat and Bang Auto Body, the Shifalo Baptist Church, Dolly's Quik Stop and, if you keep going a couple miles up the road, the Twist and Shout Bait Shop. You'll be in the neighborhood, sure enough, and drive right past Cuevastown Road, where a left turn would take you to the old Hancock North Central High School, where Brett played football for his daddy, Irvin.

There's a fancy new school now, back toward I-10 on the blacktop you'd take over to the airport. There was obviously a big to-do getting that thing built — the airport, not the high school — because the sign at the highway crossing makes you think you've arrived at O'Hare in Chicago. "Stennis International Airport and Industrial Park," the giant billboard screams. Predictably, it overstates the facility just a hair.

With all this driving around, though, and maybe enjoying a brief glimpse of the Jourdan River (waterfront lots available in Jourdan River Estates) or maybe the Bayou Laterre Hunting Club, unless you just stop and ask one of the locals, you'll wind up backtracking and trying to figure out just where this mysterious stretch of dirt and gravel called Irvin Favre Road might be hidden.

Jones: "Best way up there is to get on the Kiln-DeLisle road, which is the exit off I-10 between Kiln and Gulfport. Can't remember the number, if there is one. Anyhow, you go north past two convenience stores, turn left at the first bridge and just go straight 'til it dead-ends at Favre Road.

"You know the funny thing is, the sign there has the name spelled wrong. We joke about everybody up north not being able to pronounce Favre when they first see it — you know, they say 'F-A-R-V-E' — but heck, the county sign didn't do any better: The sign that's up there now says: Irvin Farve Road. They fouled it up, too. Probably just somebody painted it wrong. 'Course, people keep stealing the signs now that Brett's famous, so maybe when this one's gone, they'll get the next one right."

Hidden up the driveway is the Favres' version of true southern comfort: 52 acres of trees, underbrush, a creek and, yes, Rotten Bayou. The modest but comfy-looking family home sits in a clearing, just in front of the spacious party house and swimming pool that Brett contracted to be built once football had made him a man of means.

Brett also purchased 44 acres adjacent to his family's property — following long negotiations with a doctor from New Orleans — and ultimately plans to build his dream house there when he's through with football. For now, Brett's acreage across the creek from Irvin and Bonita's place is mainly grazing space for exactly seven head of cattle. That legally puts the Favres in the livestock business, which the amused Bonita runs right along with most other family enterprises.

Not that she's taking the cattle business as a joke, but the lady does have a sense of humor. In the spring of '96, at the first Brett Favre charity golf tournament, she met a man from Colorado named Dick Montfort. Bonita got a kick out of saying they discussed their mutual interest in cattle. The hoot, in case a listener doesn't get it right away, is that the Montfort Feed Lot north of Denver is home to 800,000 head. They say you can smell the Montforts in Nebraska.

Anyway, at this little Hancock County hideaway so accessible to the real world and yet somehow so far away, this piece of paradise on Rotten Bayou is where Irvin and Bonita Favre raised their four kids — Scott, Brett, Jeff and Brandi, in that order.

The boys all played football for Irvin, who coached 21 years at Hancock, and Brandi wanted to. She saw no reason why she couldn't be a quarterback like her brothers, but settled for being Miss Teen Mississippi.

The Favre kids were all achievers, all out doing something. A lot of it involved sports, a natural since Irvin had been a baseball player and coach and Bonita proudly displays a softball trophy of her own amid all the hardware Brett has collected.

Scott, who now manages Brett's properties at an upscale resort development called Diamondhead just 10 minutes from home, played quarterback at Mississippi State. Jeff was a quarterback at Hancock, too, then followed Brett to Southern Mississippi, where he avoided unfair comparisons with his famous big brother by concentrating on defense. He was a safety and a demon special-teams player.

The kids were into it as soon as they were old enough to run a few paces or throw just about anything. "They all played youth sports," Irvin said, "and we tried to follow 'em everywhere. Bonita's the one that did most of the legwork. There were times when we had four kids playing in different leagues at different times. There were a couple of times when we ended up on the wrong field, I think."

Back then, nobody was thinking about the NFL or its megabucks. And you get the sense it wouldn't have changed the family all that much if Brett had just gone on to some other line of work.

"There was a magazine story about Brett that referred to him as something like the county's favorite son," Bonita said, "and I got upset at it. I told them we don't have a 'favorite' son. Or daughter. We love 'em all just alike."

The entire setting does truly seem to jump off a Norman Rockwell canvas. The place feels like backwoods, sure enough, but it also conveys a sense of family, of peace and quiet, of old-fashioned life away from big-city America. Gulfport is maybe a 20-minute drive, New Orleans a little more than an hour, but each might as well be in a different world.

"Somebody asked me, after Brett signed a big contract, whether he was going to build us a million-dollar home," Bonita said. "I thought: Goodness, what for? What's wrong with the one we've got? It's been just fine for all of us, and now that the kids are mostly grown, a big old fancy place would just be more work for me to take care of, anyway."

There's no doubt that the old family spread is still home to Brett Favre. "It was a great place to grow up," he said, "and we've always been close, even our extended family with all the uncles and cousins and everybody. Some people look back where they were raised and they think of nice memories, but then their world changes and they move on to a whole different place.

"That's not me. To me, home is where it always was. Hey, I love Green Bay — I can't imagine playing pro football anywhere better than this — but home is Hancock County and that's where I'll wind up. Right back hanging out with the same people. Even now, with all that's going on in my life, I miss getting home. We still do things together as a family.

"Now that I'm in the NFL, I've grown to appreciate it even more because I can't be there as much as I'd like. You might not believe it, but there are times when I'm playing that I'll be on the sideline and be thinking, 'Man, I wish I was back home with everybody, watching the Saints on TV.'"

Needless to say, that's not what all those friends and kinfolk back home are doing on Sundays. They're watching the Packers, and it's quite a crowd. Growing all the time, too.

There's a big-screen television in the party room, and it's jammed with Pack rooters every week. They all bring crawfish or something else incredibly delicious to toss in the giant iron pot outside. The Favres heat that baby up all day and there's food for just about every man, woman and child in the county. Which is fine, because a whole lot of 'em are right there.

In fact, Irvin and Bonita have more or less opened their property to the world on Packer game days.

"We've got a big family anyhow," Irvin said. "There're Favres all over this part of Mississippi. I do think we've picked up a few more relatives since Brett got to the NFL, but that's OK. Everybody's welcome."

And yes, Packer fans all the way from Wisconsin have, indeed, survived all the wrong turns and confusing directions to find 1213 Irvin Favre Road. "Strangers turn up at our place pretty regularly now," Bonita said. "We had one wonderful couple from Wisconsin show up here for a game one time. They were really nice people, and we told 'em just grab some food out of the pot and join the gang. I think they had the time of their lives with all us crazy country people hollering at the TV set."

By the way, on the subject of Brett's home, there has been considerable confusion among the national media about the pronunciation of Kiln. Which, in that part of Mississippi, folks call "The Kiln." Why? Nobody knows. They also call Pass Christian, "The Pass."

Anyway, announcers stumbled over Kiln when Favre was a kid quarterback just emerging onto the NFL scene, and finally the Packer publicity people straightened everyone out. They asked Brett and then decreed that the town's name is pronounced, "*Kill*."

Which is true. Except that there's this other tiny detail. Kiln isn't really where the Favres live.

"Oh man, here we go again on the hometown thing," Irvin Favre said. "By now, all the guys on TV say he's from Kiln and that's OK, 'cause it's right down the road. When the Gulfport paper did a special section on Brett after he won the MVP thing, they put a headline on the front that called him, "Kiln-Billy." It's not a big deal, but our property really isn't in Kiln. It's in Fenton."

So the media in Green Bay and elsewhere should change Brett's residence to Fenton?

"Well, actually," Bonita said, "Fenton doesn't have a post office. It's like a little bitty area sort of east from Kiln. Our mailing address is actually Pass Christian. Of course, people send us stuff and it'll get here whether you send it to Pass, or Kiln, or wherever. Everybody around here knows where we are."

But that doesn't answer the question about Brett's official, honest-to-goodness hometown. For the sake of accuracy, what is it?

"He's got a home in Diamondhead now," Bonita said, introducing yet another name into the mix. "But Diamondhead is really Pass Christian, too. I know that when Brett went up to play at Southern Miss, they listed his home as Pass Christian. That's probably the most accurate, but it's not like we worry about it. Kiln's fine. It was fun hearing people trying to pronounce it."

Indeed, why start another round of sports anchors tripping over their tongues? It would take another full football season for everyone to learn, *"Paz Christianne."*

Actually, the Favres consider the entire fuss over Brett's hometown kind of funny. To everyone in the family, he's still a great kid — but nothing to get all silly over. Irvin and Bonita remember more about Brett's days fishing for crawfish, climbing trees and shooting BB guns with his brothers than they do about last year's games against the Chicago Bears.

"I wish I had a nickel for every window that got shot out," Irvin said.

Bonita recalled that while Brett was certainly a normal southern country boy, he probably wasn't going to spend a lot of time firing guns at the abundant local animal population. "I think he went out one morning, all bundled up because it was kind of cold, and he was going deer hunting," she said. "On the other side of the creek, I guess he came right up on a deer, and it scared both of them to death. You know, one of those things where Brett ran one way and the deer ran the other way. That's when I knew he probably wasn't really going to be much into hunting."

Like all his siblings, though, Brett *was* into sports.

"It wasn't like he was this great natural talent that just stuck out," Irvin said. "But he could play, and he was always a hard-nosed kid. I had him playing quarterback and safety for me as a junior and senior in high school (Brett had mononucleosis as a sophomore), and you could tell he had a head for the game. And obviously, he had a heck of an arm. He played baseball, too, and he was a real good player. Pitched and played shortstop, mostly.

"I coached the legion team here for a long time, and we had some really good ballclubs. Now that people are writing stories about Brett in the NFL, they all bring up that I was a football coach for so long, but really, in this part of Mississippi, I was probably better known for the tough baseball teams we had. And Brett was one of the real good ones I coached."

Doug Barber, a sports writer for the newspaper in Gulfport, remembered Brett from his high school days, and insisted that nobody could possibly have guessed that he'd wind up in the NFL. "He was a good athlete, but not the kind of guy who just stands out to where scouts come from all over to look at him," Barber said. "Not at all. Matter of fact, if you had told me back then that Brett Favre from Hancock County would make it as a famous athlete, I'd have guessed it would have been in baseball. He could hit, and obviously, he could throw."

One of Barber's colleagues, photographer Tim Isbell, recalled turning out to shoot an American Legion game in which Brett was going to play shortstop. "I was just standing around over behind first base before the game," Isbell said. "They were taking infield practice, and Brett turned loose this wild throw that I never saw coming. It hit me right in the chest. That's not something you forget. It left a pretty good bruise.

"I remember Brett yelling over to say he was sorry he hit me."

That was one of young Favre's rare apologies, particularly on the baseball field.

"I loved to pitch," Brett said. "I could always throw hard, even though I never really worked on technique or anything like that. I just aimed and threw. Hard as I could. One game, I think I struck out 15 guys, but I also hit maybe three batters right in a row. I guess some of the hitters got pretty nervous up there, but I thought that was great. It just made me want to throw harder."

Much later, after he'd squeezed out a football scholarship at Southern Mississippi, Brett considered playing both sports at the collegiate level. By then, the coaches believed he was a genuine prospect at each.

"I was actually planning to play ball in the spring of my freshman year," Favre said, "but then I made the No. 1 quarterback in the fall. When I got to be a starter right away, and had some success, I decided I'd better get serious and learn all I could about football and stick with that. So when spring came, I was at football practice instead of playing baseball. It was the right decision, but sometimes I wonder what I could have done if I'd played baseball."

One of Brett's traits, right from boyhood, was that he

was stubborn as a mule. He's referred to it again and again, even as a pro football player, and how it's gotten him in trouble with coaches and other authority figures.

Ask Mike Holmgren. Or back in Mississippi, ask Irvin Favre.

"Brett led a drive to win a big football game one night," Irvin said. "We got behind and we had to throw the ball more than I usually liked to do (which was rarely, at best). Anyway, he got us down the field, right to the 1-yard line, and I called an off-tackle play.

"Well, Brett saw something the way the other team was lined up and he just ignored my call. He ran a quarterback sneak, and he scored. Everybody was jumping up and down celebrating, and meanwhile I ran down near the end zone and we got into an argument all the way back to the bench."

Never mind that the play worked for the winning touchdown.

"I wanted him to respect the coach's decision," Irvin said, still as bull-headed about the call today as he was on that Friday night years ago. "We had a certain way I wanted things done, and that way had worked for a long time, and I didn't want a young kid going against my calls. It didn't matter that it was my own boy, except maybe I was even madder."

Brett Favre the pro football star has become renowned for his toughness, his hard-nosed approach to the game in an era when quarterbacks typically are being protected like precious works of art. Spend one day with Irvin Favre and there's no question where Brett's hardest, roughest, do-it-my-way, never-quit, knock-the-guy-down attitude comes from.

Irvin is built like a Coke machine with an extra-short, flat-top haricut, perhaps one of the last left in America. He's got that rugged countenance and perpetual scowl of a Marine drill sergeant, or a lifetime football man. Just a quick look and you know that Irvin Favre probably isn't a man you'd want to sass, and his coaching philosophy is certainly going to be: "My way or the highway."

Not likely that you'd think of Irvin as a '90s kind of guy. Maybe his boy is making millions running fancy-pants "West Coast" offense, but Irvin's teams ran the ball down your throat and planted you on your backside. If Woody Hayes had been born in bayou country down near the Gulf, he'd have been Irvin Favre.

So if Irvin's son risks life and limb trying to run over a linebacker for that extra two yards, nobody should be surprised. If he makes outrageous demands on himself, works like a dog and refuses to step away from any sort of challenge...hey, that's what any of Irvin's kids were *supposed* to do.

But then there's Brett's other side, the make-it-up-as-you-go individualist. No question he got that from Bonita's side of the family.

The former Bonita French was a special education teacher most of her professional career, working with slow or disadvantaged students. "I did all kinds of things I wasn't supposed to," she said. "I'd take the kids into grocery stores so they'd get some exposure to everyday things that maybe they wouldn't have any other way. One time, I took a class of Special Ed kids on a ferry boat ride. I didn't have permission to do it, and Lord knows what would have happened if one of them had fallen overboard or something.

"I just thought: These kids probably won't ever have a chance to do this if I don't take them myself. And I knew if I asked ahead of time, somebody would tell me I couldn't do it. So I just went ahead anyway. It was a great experience."

And nobody fell off the boat.

Bonita likewise came by her flamboyant independence honestly. It ran way back; for instance, her dad Benny ran an infamous gambling saloon in Pass Christian before any kind of gaming was legal in Mississippi.

When some sports writer goes into the cliche book after an outrageous, on-the-spot play and comes up with a description of Brett as a riverboat gambler, he's hitting closer to home that he'll ever know.

"And then there's my mom (Icella)," Bonita said. "She's the real free spirit in the whole bunch. Since Brett's gotten famous and where we live has started making people curious, well, it's natural that a few will show up to poke around. Most of the time, we don't mind — especially on Sundays, when everybody's invited to come watch football. But it's not like we want to give away all our privacy, either. Irvin and I aren't thrilled with opening the place up like Graceland.

"Do you think that bothers Mom? People show up, she

just pops out there, says hi and conducts a tour. Doesn't matter if it's 7 o'clock in the morning. She'll bring folks right into the house. No kidding, you've got to be careful what you're wearing when you walk through the kitchen in the morning. Mom's liable to be finished pointing out Brett's trophy cases and decided to show some tourists what's in the refrigerator. Honestly."

Bonita Favre laughed as she told the story about her mother. "It runs in the family," she said. "If anybody wonders how Brett can be such an independent soul sometimes, well, I suppose they could just come see us and they'd understand."

Yes, they would.

Visiting the Favres, traveling the back roads of Hancock County, chatting up a few fellows at the Quik Stop, sitting a spell on the dock looking into the murky depths of Rotten Bayou, wandering the clumpy grass at old North Central High — the whole picture begins to come into focus.

As Frank Winters said, "Once you get past thinking about the gators and snakes and all of that, visiting Brett right down there where he grew up tells you a lot.

"Some people just come from a place. Brett *is* that place."

CHAPTER FOUR:
JUST A SLOW WHITE BOY

It's pretty hard to imagine the NFL's most valuable player being almost totally anonymous in high school.

Hard, but not impossible.

Just ask Green Bay Packers' record-setting quarterback, who was so unknown entering his junior year of prep football that he was barely even mentioned in the local newspaper's preseason special edition. You can look it up: The *Sun Herald* in Gulfport not only carries features on all the projected stars around the Mississippi Gulf Coast, but runs thumbnail sketches on every team.

If you scrounge around long enough, deep into the scouting report on Hancock North Central for 1985, you'll find one sentence in the 10th paragraph: "Running the attack is junior Brett Favre (6-2, 185), who did not play football last year."

That's it.

Prior to any mention of this new signal-caller, the story

noted that Hancock, which had suffered through a 4-6 season in '84, would be returning to the wishbone offense that had been so successful at the school in the late 1970s.

Coach Irvin Favre, the new quarterback's father, was quoted this way: "Our glory years were when we ran the wishbone, and we have some real exciting people in the backfield. (Up front) we've got some good-sized kids. This may be the biggest line since I've been here."

The "exciting" backs the coach talked about were Drew Malley, Stanley Jordan, Donald Vince and especially the swift and elusive 155-pound Charles Burton, for whom great things were predicted.

The elder Favre didn't really have anything out of the ordinary to say about his boy Brett. Maybe Irvin Favre mentioned in passing that Brett missed his sophomore year because he'd suffered through a bout of mononucleosis, or perhaps the coach hinted that Brett had a strong arm and a little potential.

But if Irvin did, it didn't make the newspaper.

And that's the fanfare this future all-pro received as he began his high school career. Oh, and just to add to the notion that young Brett's tenure at Hancock wasn't destined to be anything spectacular, his very first game — at St. John — was cancelled in the aftermath of Hurricane Elena.

Some start.

Now the next segment of any rags-to-riches saga normally would be about the quarterback's incredible development in high school: how he grew five inches, learned the proper throwing technique and began scattering touchdown passes to every corner of the state.

That didn't happen, either.

Coach Favre made good on his promise to run the ball the entire two years his son played quarterback. Wishbone the first season, Wing-T and Power-I the second. And sure enough, Charles Burton made all-coast as a senior by rushing for more than 1,000 yards and scoring 20 touchdowns.

"When we were in high school, we didn't have that many pass plays and stuff like that," Burton said. "We always had good backs, like Stanley, Drew, Delano Lewis, Donald, Brett and myself. We never did have to throw too many passes."

Favre's role seemed to be dutifully working at operating this power offense efficiently. "Brett didn't have to do that much," Burton said. "But when we'd run the Wing-T and Power-I in practice, he'd want to get it done and get it done right. He didn't leave the practice field until the coaches were happy."

Hard worker, tough competitor, no numbers.

Truth is, if he'd just gone off and gotten a job when he was 18, Brett Favre would have been remembered back home as a pretty decent quarterback, but an even better strong safety who made the all-area team and played in the state all-star game his senior year primarily because of his prowess on defense.

The irony isn't lost on Brett, who mentioned it right after he won the MVP award in 1995.

"I didn't see the list (of previous winners) until the day

the award came out," he said. "Our PR guy showed it to me. It's pretty impressive. When you look at it, there aren't many surprises. Nearly all of them were big stars at big schools. When somebody like Emmitt Smith or Steve Young wins the MVP, nobody is really surprised because they're kind of expected to do those things.

"To tell you the truth, that makes it a little more special. I saw on SportsCenter that most MVPs were dominant players at the high school and college levels. But in high school, I was no different than the quarterback at Bay High or St. Stanislaus or Pearl River Central.

"Heck, I was third string in the high school all-star game. Looking back on it now, I'm kind of glad it was that way."

Really, one of the near-miracles in the Brett Favre story is that he was recruited at all, let alone awarded the very last scholarship available at his father's alma mater, the University of Southern Mississippi just up the road at Hattiesburg.

The man responsible for that virtually impossible turn of events was Mark McHale, the Southern Miss offensive line coach whose recruiting territory just happened to include Hancock County. And to make the tale even better, McHale hadn't been on the Southern Miss staff during Favre's junior season, which meant that the primary prospect list for the 1987 freshman class had been drawn up without his input.

Needless to say, Brett Favre wasn't on it.

After all, Hancock North Central had run up a 6-4

Brett is remembered as a big-game player at Hancock North Central, but he ran the ball about as often as he threw it during his two high school seasons.

record in '85, and Favre threw a grand total of 97 passes in 10 games, completing only 40 for 723 yards and eight touchdowns. Those aren't exactly the kind of numbers that bring college coaches swarming into the county.

Think of some other future pro stars and try to imagine the mobs following them around by the time they've completed their junior years in high school.

Dan Marino? Steve Young? Troy Aikman? With quarterbacks of that caliber, every coach in the nation knows the kid's whole family all the way out to third cousins by the time the boy is a sophomore. When he's a junior or senior, there are so many recruiters hanging around that you can't find a motel room within 50 miles on game nights.

But Brett Favre? Well, he was there for the taking. No problem bumping into other recruiters. There were plenty of good seats available.

"I got to Hattiesburg for the '86 season," McHale said, "and the way college recruiting works, the basic decisions are made the previous spring. The staff puts its top guys on the board, and then in the fall, you're basically just out double-checking people to see how the players on your wish list are coming along. You're screening people out, so to speak. Who's moving up or down, who's gotten hurt, who's committed to some other school, that sort of thing."

Which is what McHale was doing at the start of the 1986 season, except that when he was wandering through his area down around the Gulf Coast, people kept mentioning this kid he'd never seen and knew for a fact wasn't even on the prospect chart.

"To be honest, you get to talking to head coaches and assistants at some of the schools you cover," McHale recalled, "and somebody would say, 'Have you seen that quarterback at Hancock North Central?' I had to say no, I hadn't.

"Frankly, the way they were describing Brett, he sounded like a slow white boy who was just a pretty good athlete. But you hear that about a lot of kids, and they just aren't capable of playing football at the Division I level.

"But it was funny. I heard the same thing about this quarterback at a second school, and then at a third, and finally I figured maybe I better have a look. I mean, you don't want to make a big mistake and have to admit you never even *saw* a guy.

"So I got hold of Irvin, who of course had played baseball at USM and really wanted Brett to come up there. He told me he thought the boy could play college ball, so I agreed to come over and see him.

"Well, I get there and Irvin hands me this tape. I pop the thing in and it was all running plays. The three or four throws Brett made were play-action passes that any kid could have completed. I told Irvin, 'There's no way I can take this back and show it to anybody. They don't want to watch a tape of a quarterback handing off on a sprint draw.'

"Besides that, Brett didn't look very fast. I met the boy — I remember this little bitty shed thing they had to work out in — and you know Brett. He came up and said, 'Coach, Coach, I can play for you. I *know* I can.'

"Anyway, I went down there for a game, and of course

I'm thinking Irvin knows I'm scouting his son, so he's going to let him throw the ball. I watched Brett warm up, real close, and I could see he had lots of pop on the ball. It was obvious that he had a great arm. That was the first time I said, 'Hey, I like this.'

"But don't you know? Then comes the game and I think Brett threw three passes. So I had to go back and ask Irvin what the heck was going on. Didn't he realize I couldn't talk up a kid who was just handing off the ball? So Irvin says, 'Look, come back one more time and I promise we'll open it up. We will.' "

McHale admitted that, with all the other prospects he had to see — not to mention his regular coaching duties at USM — he might have given the Favre kid up as a lost cause. Except he'd seen that arm. That magic arm.

"OK, so somehow I find the time to go back and watch Hancock a *second* time," McHale said. "Probably some other coaches on our staff wondered what in the world I was doing. But Irvin promised he'd let Brett throw the ball. And he did. Four times instead of three.

"I was about ready to go down on the sideline myself, except that after three little short passes that didn't mean anything, Brett let go of that fourth one and I'll remember it all my life like it happened five minutes ago. He rolled out to the right hash mark and just zoomed the ball 60 yards to the end zone.

"I'm telling you, that football had smoke and fire coming off it. The thing about drove a hole in this little receiver's chest. I saw that and decided then and there that Brett was a big, big-time possibility. He had no experience in a passing offense but — my, oh my — God only gives out so many arms like that.

"You know, there's another thing about all this: Coach (Jim) Carmody was the head coach at USM then and the school had had its biggest years running the option with Reggie Collier at quarterback. Reggie was blinding fast with a good arm, and they'd gone to some bowl games, so everybody was out looking for another Reggie Collier.

"Believe me, I knew Brett Favre wouldn't be running any option offense. He couldn't run at all. But in the back of my mind, I was always thinking that, in a program like Southern Miss, if you don't have a Reggie Collier — and we definitely weren't going to find another one — you'd better start figuring on throwing the ball if you plan to score. So I went back up to Hattiesburg, made my pitch and got Brett onto the recruiting board. At the very bottom."

Meanwhile, as Brett's status with the staff at Southern Miss was upgraded from non-entity to a very remote possibility, he was busy having a very eventful season. In fact, with Burton and Co. running the ball and Brett throwing only when necessary, the Hawks won their first seven games and crept up to a No. 9 ranking in the state.

The seventh victory was a doozy, on the road against Long Beach, and it will be remembered as long as they play football in Hancock County, Mississippi.

Favre was a force from the beginning, running 25 yards for the first touchdown on, of all things, an option keeper.

Then he tacked on a 6-yard TD pass to Vincent Cuevas and a two-point conversion throw to Casey Hood, making it 14-0.

Long Beach cut the deficit to 14-7, then Burton got loose on a 47-yard scoring dash with Brett tossing another two-point conversion pass for a 22-7 lead.

But on the next series, Burton was whistled for a personal foul and thrown out of the game. "When the refs kicked me out," Burton said, "Brett walked up to me and said, 'Don't worry, big brother, we will win the game.' "

To do it, Favre had to display — for the first time — the type of last-gasp heroics fans at Southern Miss and now in Green Bay have come to take for granted. In a sense, this would turn into a coming-out party for the real Brett Favre.

In Burton's absence, Long Beach seized the momentum and scored twice to tie the game 22-22. Hancock was floundering, until the Hawks got possession one last time on their own 41-yard line with 59 seconds to play — and Favre in serious pain.

"I had cramps in both legs," he said. "I couldn't move. I think at the end, everybody was expecting that we'd wind up tied."

Yet Brett somehow cranked up his team for the final drive, completing passes for 16 yards to Tim Cox and 12 more to Frank Miller. Hancock had reached the Long Beach 4-yard line, and despite his cramps, Brett ran another option, bulling to the 1-yard line. "I figured I would have to pitch it," he said, "but I didn't want to leave it on the ground so I kept it."

And then he called his own number again, on the play Irvin Favre remembers so well as nothing short of outright disobedience, and scored the winning touchdown with 28 seconds remaining. Brett collapsed after crossing the goal line.

However angry Irvin might have been at Brett's play change, he admitted the whole drive was an amazing feat. "Brett played just a super football game," the coach said afterward. "Maybe the best he's ever played. God, we're just tremendously happy. Brett ran hard, threw and played defense. It was real tough on him, but he's a real competitor."

The passing explosion against Long Beach even amazed the teammates who knew Brett best. But most weren't surprised.

"We always knew the potential was there," running back Stanley Jordan said. "He had an exceptionally strong arm. I feel like if we had thrown the ball more, we'd have been just as successful."

Cuevas, who caught a TD pass that night against Long Beach, wondered if he'd ever see the Favre gun unleashed at Hancock. "Brett was a year ahead of me and I ended up catching at least eight touchdown passes," Cuevas said. "In high school, his dad got on him in practice. The pass would hit you and you couldn't hardly catch it. His dad told him to take something off the ball. But that showed how much arm strength he had in high school.

"It's a great honor to know I played with him. A lot of

people are jealous of him, but I know what kind of leadership he had in high school."

Jordan also recalled Favre's toughness. Asked to single out one play that stuck in his memory, Jordan said, "We were playing Stone High up here at Perkinston and he threw an interception. Brett looked like a heat-seeking guided missile. He tackled the guy and nearly killed the individual. He really had blood in his eyes."

Burton, whose running skills kept passing to a minimum, made a prediction that turned out to be truer than he ever could have guessed. "On the day we left high school," Burton said, "I told Brett I knew he could make it as a quarterback. Brett was throwing the ball 50 and 60 yards in the ninth grade. I remember when we beat Pearl River with 35 seconds to go on a prayer. He can really throw a ball."

Hancock North Central finished 8-2 Brett's final year, losing to local powerhouse d'Iberville 28-6 for the District VIII, Class 4-A title. But the Hawks, notwithstanding that one wild night against Long Beach, had been a running team and so the quarterback went largely unnoticed by college recruiters.

Except Mark McHale.

"Remember, we put Brett on our board at the very bottom," McHale said. "But every year, for whatever reason, that list starts to thin out. Guys play their way off, some don't make grades, some decide to go somewhere else. So the list gets shorter and shorter, and that year, Brett just stayed on it and moved up, little by little.

photo by University of Southern Mississippi Sports Information Department

Mark McHale

"I kept pushing him every chance I got, and finally it got down to where it looked like we'd have one scholarship left. We had a staff meeting, and I banged on the table talking about Brett, and then somebody asked me: 'Can he play free safety?'

"Now, there's no way at all Brett Favre could have been a free safety at the level we're talking about. No way at all. I was probably just a big ol' dumb guy trying to get myself fired, but for whatever reason, I said, 'Heck, yeah, he can play free safety. He'll start by the time he's a sophomore.'

"I probably never told a bigger lie in my life."

Still, the Favres had to sweat it out. Blue-chip recruits get the royal treatment during their official campus visits, but when the Favre family at last was asked to come to Hattiesburg, the result was something of an embarrassment.

"Brett was all excited," McHale said, "but honestly, the staff wasn't paying much attention. I mean, this was the bottom guy, the last name. I felt for Irvin and Bonita. They had to wait in the lobby and it seemed like nobody did anything about them like they would for some important recruit. It felt to me like they were wanting this so bad, and here they were just sitting around for what must have been forever."

Thamus Coleman, a longtime coach and now football administrative assistant who has been at Southern Miss for 19 years, recalled how stubborn McHale became when that last scholarship seemed to be up for grabs.

"Mark just kept saying we ought to take Brett, that he could play other positions if he couldn't make it at quarterback," Coleman said. "Well now, Mark surely knew better, but he'd seen the boy throw and the other coaches hadn't, and I think Mark figured that if he could somehow get Brett onto campus and on that practice field, the rest would take care of itself.

"I'm not sure but that they didn't give Brett the scholarship at the end just because his dad was an alum, and maybe they wanted to keep the lines open down in that part of the state. Be pretty tough to get anyone to admit that now, because from the first time Brett threw a football here in Hattiesburg — he was 17 years old — that thing came zinging, buddy."

"Brett went from the bottom of the ladder to the main guy of Southern Miss football about as quick as he gets rid of the football, and that's pretty quick."

Favre appreciates how long the odds really were.

"If there was ever an example of someone who defied the odds, it was me," he said. "I'd look around at the people Coast schools have sent to major colleges, and I'd say, 'No way. This is just not a place that puts out pro athletes.' But I never gave up. I kept believing because the one thing you don't ever want to do is look back and say, 'I wish.' Look back and say, 'I'm glad I did not once cheat myself.'"

So as it turned out, Irvin Favre had been right all along. His son *could* play quarterback in college, even if daddy hadn't let him pass it much in high school. And Brett was right when he was jumping up and down and telling McHale, "Coach, I can play for you."

But most of all, McHale was right for sticking to his guns. He believed his eyes instead of conventional wisdom.

"Having some role in Brett's chance to develop into what he's become gives me as much satisfaction as anything I've done in my career," McHale said. "Not so much because Brett's gone on to be a star in the pros and all that. No, mostly it makes me so happy because it's a great family and this has always been one super kid.

"I still get excited for him. One year when the Packers played the Saints in New Orleans, I went over for the game. I never expected to see Brett, because I didn't want to bother him, but after the game, while he had this big crowd of media and cameras and such all around, somehow he saw me.

"Brett just stopped talking right in mid-sentence, looked straight at me and got this big smile. 'Hey, Coach McHale!' he said, and I thought: He's still the same good boy I know. It's a wonderful story, and I'm thrilled I was a part of it.

"Sometimes I think, now that I've left Southern Miss for a few years and come back (for the 1996 season), that maybe I ought to go back down there to that old field at Hancock. Just stand there and imagine that kid throwing the football.

"I'll never see anything like it again, I'll tell you. Maybe nobody will."

CHAPTER FIVE:
COACH, I'M READY

Comparisons between Brett Favre and John Elway really aren't all that surprising.

Both quarterbacks have bazooka arms. They're each strong, tough and resourceful, perhaps most dangerous when a play breaks down and they're left to scramble around surveying the field. And even though Favre hasn't been in the NFL nearly as long as the Denver bomber, he's already shown a lot of that legendary Elway flair for fourth-quarter heroics.

It is, however, a bit of a shock to learn that the first time Favre heard anything about similarities to Elway, Brett was a 17-year old freshman at Southern Mississippi — and a third-stringer, to boot.

And that the guys who linked the two passers were on the other side of the line of scrimmage.

"It's pretty hard to forget the start of our summer practice in 1987," said Thamus Coleman, who has been on the football staff at Southern Miss for nearly two decades. "The freshmen come in early, you know, and the veterans report a little later.

"To tell you the truth, maybe that's the only way this could have happened the way it did. But Brett was just this raw kid from down in Hancock County — he was recruited as a defensive back, honestly — and nobody really thought anything about him.

"But then, he was around with the other freshmen and the coaches watched him throw the ball a few times. And I'm goin' to tell you, it was pretty hard to believe. So they moved him over to quarterback, and this is the truth: He was just a baby, and never played in any kind of passing offense, but the first time that boy walked into a huddle on campus, he moved the football.

"It's funny thinking about it. Coaches would stop what they were doing and just look over from wherever they were. I mean, Brett walked out there from the first day and it was like he'd been doin' this all his life. He could see every inch of the field, he knew every route, he just zinged the ball to receivers. It was unbelievable."

Soon enough, the Southern Miss vets arrived in camp and the pace picked up. Once the big boys get involved, everything happens quicker as better and older athletes make plays the recruits and walk-ons have never even dreamed about. So Favre, naturally, was penciled in as the No. 3 quarterback, which is a tough spot because only the first- and second-unit guys get any serious work.

"But the way Brett threw the ball," assistant coach Mark

McHale recalled, "he was pretty hard to ignore, so eventually they stuck him in a scrimmage where he was probably facing the No. 2 defense. And he still looked good.

"Finally, in another scrimmage, I can't remember which guys he had with him, but the coaches wanted to see him play against our first-unit defense — he's only 17 now and never been in any kind of situation like that. But doggone it, he'd get in the huddle and just take over and he started just firin' the ball.

"Well, our defensive guys couldn't believe it, either, and they all started chanting, 'EL-way! EL-way! EL-way.' Right about then, the head coach (Jim Carmody) says, 'You know what? If a kid impresses my own defense that darn much, maybe I've gotta get him in there.' "

It should be noted that Carmody, who was beginning his sixth and ultimately final season as the Southern Miss coach, wasn't really looking for a passer when Favre showed up on campus. The Golden Eagles had enjoyed some success playing option football, particularly from 1979-82, a span in which they compiled a 31-13-2 record with the multi-talented Reggie Collier running the attack.

But the supply of option quarterbacks had worn thin, and Carmody faced a dilemma in '87. He didn't really have the horses to stick with a ground game, and since Southern Miss hadn't been out recruiting passers, it seemed futile to consider switching philosophies at the last minute.

And then along came Favre.

Wide receiver Robbie Weeks, who had been doing a lot more blocking than catching footballs his first two years in

Hattiesburg, recalled the coaches' sudden change of heart. "It was like Brett stood out right away," Weeks said. "Of course, he was on the scout team (the No. 3 unit) to begin with, and most of the rest of us probably didn't even realize he was there to begin with. But it sure didn't take long.

"We'd watch Brett and say, 'Hey, who *is* this guy?' You know, with somebody who can throw the ball like that, he's usually a big-name prospect and everybody's waiting to see him. But I was from Indianola, in another part of the state, and I'd never even heard of Brett Favre.

"That changed in a hurry. He could just dad-gum *sling* the ball!"

The always-cocksure Favre, in fact, was hoping that he might actually get to play in the 1987 season opener against Alabama. Brett went to McHale, the offensive line coach who had recruited him — and had become something of a father confessor — and told him, "I'm ready, I'm ready." McHale could only tell the boy to stay prepared and hope for the best.

"Heck, as the No. 3 man, Brett wasn't getting any of the repetitions in practice," McHale said. "No work at all with the regulars on the game plan. He just practiced all week with the scout team, and so we went over to Birmingham and Alabama really thumped us (38-6). We not only didn't move the ball on offense, it looked like we never *would* move it."

Southern Miss had its home opener coming up the next week against Tulane, and Carmody was facing some heat. Losing to Alabama is never a disgrace, obviously, but the

The fresh-faced youngster ready to take on the world at Southern Mississippi.

Eagles had looked toothless and there were serious questions raised about how they were going to score any points. To everyone's surprise, Carmody told the media at his weekly press gathering that he was considering taking a look at this freshman Favre kid, maybe even in the Tulane game.

"What was so strange about that," McHale said, "was that Coach mentioned the possibility that Brett might play a little, but he was still No. 3 all week and didn't get any game preparation at all. I was worried that if something happened and Coach did throw Brett in there for a series or two, heck, he might be completely lost without being prepped for it."

Favre had no such qualms. Once again he went to McHale, this time in the locker room as the Eagles were about to take the field, and announced, "Coach, I'm ready."

McHale said: "I could see how excited he was, and I told him, 'Look, son, I know you're ready to go, and I promise there's a good chance you'll get in the game.' Well, just as I said that, I looked around and Coach (Carmody) was standing right behind me. I figured I might have just gotten myself fired for telling Brett what I did."

No chance. Instead, McHale turned into a prophet.

Junior Ailrick Young started at quarterback for Southern Miss, which led 7-3 at half-time despite not getting much done offensively. Tulane rallied to go up 10-7, then the Eagles got a tying field goal early in the third quarter as backup QB Simmie Carter replaced Young. Still, the attack was sputtering — the Eagles advanced just 16 yards after an interception prior to Chris Seroka's field goal.

When Tulane scored again to make it 16-10 and Young couldn't move the ball on the next Southern Miss series, Carmody decided to take the plunge. He turned to Favre and said, "Warm up."

McHale: "You should have seen Brett. He was hopping up and down on the sideline like a Mexican jumping bean."

Most of the Southern Miss players were surprised, despite what they'd seen in practice. "Personally, I didn't expect to see Brett in the game," Weeks said. "I thought they were grooming him for the next year, that they were going to red-shirt him."

Center Jim Ferrell assumed the same thing. "We had seen Brett in practice and we knew what he could do," Ferrell said, "but we knew he was a true freshman and we didn't expect him to come in. We just thought it was going to be another long game."

Instead, the 16,023 witnesses at Roberts Stadium were privileged to sit in on a bit of history.

Carmody made the call with 9:35 left in the third quarter, and Favre trotted onto the field. Despite all his pregame bravado, Brett admitted he was a bundle of nerves. "I was scared," he said. "It was quite an experience running out there. When I went in, I just didn't know where to throw the ball. My mind felt like it was blown. So I just kept the ball and ran."

Favre's first keeper went for no gain, but then he completed his first collegiate pass, a 7-yarder to Eugene

Rowell on third down. The Eagles had to punt, but Favre had survived his brief case of jitters and Southern Miss football would never be the same.

On Brett's second series, he showed some of the skills that have served him so well ever since — and handed USM a 17-16 lead in the process. Brett finished off a drive with a 7-yard touchdown pass to Chris McGee that was pure improvisation.

"That was a drop-back pass," Favre said. "It was a busted play. The rush came in so I rolled out. Chris' man fell down, so I lofted it out and hoped he'd catch it. He did."

"The cornerback ran into his own man and left me free," McGee said. "Give credit to Brett Favre. He made a hellacious move on the blitz to get away and throw it to me."

Before the afternoon was over, Favre had directed two more scoring drives. Ultimately, his 23-yard TD pass to Alfred Williams proved decisive in the Eagles' 31-24 victory.

"Brett came in and was the spark," Ferrell said. "In his second series, we knew all we had to do was hold them out and we were going down the field. He sparked us, we got a roll going and we burned the house down."

That victory over Tulane turned out to be the first of several torch jobs Favre engineered during four spectacular seasons at Southern Miss.

The third-stringer who showed up as an unknown defensive back went on to throw for 7,695 yards and 52 touchdowns, leading the Eagles to bowl games following the 1988 and '90 seasons. Along the way, he racked up the top six individual passing games in school history, became USM's all-time career leader in total offense and engineered several stunning upsets that rocked the college football universe.

Favre's uniform No. 4 was retired by Southern Miss in 1993 — he was only the second player so honored — and the number now hangs outside Roberts Stadium in the university's Walk of Fame.

Looking back, Favre hears all the talk about his first-year swagger, his unwavering coolness under fire right from his initial practice as a freshman — and he can only shake his head.

"I remember being very nervous (starting college ball)," he said. "It's probably the most nervous I've ever been, including my first NFL game. I'm normally a confident guy, but there was some doubt there. I didn't know what to expect. I was afraid I was going to do something to embarrass myself.

"If you had told me then that nine years later, I would be the MVP of the National Football League, I would have laughed in your face and said, 'You're crazy.' I wouldn't have believed it. Like a lot of kids, I grew up dreaming of playing in the NFL, but at that moment, it was the furthest thing from my mind. I was just hoping to be the third-string quarterback so I could make the travel squad.

"Later on, once I started playing in college, I got the chance to look at other quarterbacks and I began to realize that I matched up with them pretty well. All of a sudden, I started thinking: 'Hey, maybe I can be pretty good.' "

Mission accomplished, and then some. Favre actually altered the landscape of Southern Mississippi football.

"What was really great for Southern Miss was that because of Brett, they changed the offense completely," Weeks said. "They'd had that option-type offense in the past, but for us to win, we had to start throwing the ball and it happened with Brett.

"There's a couple things I remember most about Brett in college, and I'll bet the guys he plays with now in Green Bay would say the same thing. First of all, he was always loose and confident. It was like he knew he could get it done. He'd keep you laughing in the huddle. When things got tough, he was always the one who picked us up. He just never panicked. He played like he'd been out there his whole life.

"The other thing, which everybody knows about now, is how he throws the ball. He had a super-quick release, for one thing. You wondered how he could throw the ball so hard without winding up. From the first time we worked together, I knew right away that I could *never* outrun his passes, so you always kept going as far as you could.

"You never knew where he was going to throw it, either. It was like everybody was the primary receiver, because he could see the whole field. On every play, you had to run a route like the ball was coming to you. If you ever went out there and weren't paying attention, he could make you look like a fool accidentally.

"There was never time to change gears or anything. When he decided he let the ball go, it got to you in a hurry,

photo by University of Southern Mississippi Sports Information Department

Favre was a student of the game right from the beginning, discussing strategy with assistant coach Gerald Goodman during Brett's freshman season.

with some serious zip. You'd run a route and turn in or something, and go, 'Wow, there it is.' It was kind of funny sometimes because we'd play teams that hadn't faced Brett before and you'd see the cornerbacks and safeties get together like, 'What happened? How'd it get there?' "

Southern Miss still didn't have waves of blue-chip monsters up front in those years, but with Favre at the trigger, the Eagles were dangerous every week. Florida State, Auburn and Alabama each felt the upset sting before Favre was done at Hattiesburg.

The Eagles went 6-5 during Brett's freshman year, including a three-game winning streak at midseason that included satisfying victories over Mississippi State — on a last-minute, 99-yard drive — and Memphis State. Southern Miss averaged almost 27 points per game once Favre was installed as the full-time quarterback, but a sometimes-porous defense led to 34-24 and 37-30 losses to Northeast Louisiana and Southwestern Louisiana, respectively — and Carmody paid for it with his job.

Curley Hallman came aboard as head coach in 1988, but perhaps even more important for Favre's development as a future superstar, Jeff Bower returned to his alma mater as offensive coordinator. Ironically, former quarterback Bower holds just about the only record Favre didn't break during his four-year bombing raid. Bower still clings to the USM mark for total offense in a single game (376 yards against Texas-Arlington in 1973).

"I always made sure Coach Hallman got Brett out of games before he could get my record," Bower joked. "You don't want to be taking your offensive coordinator out of the books."

Bower masterminded the Eagles' offense during the 1988 and '89 seasons, and Favre essentially went wild those two years. In '88, as Southern Miss rolled to a 10-2 record, averaged 30 points per game and captured a 38-18 Independence Bowl victory over Texas-El Paso, Favre threw for 2,271 yards and 16 touchdowns. The next year, USM finished a disappointing 5-6 — once again because there just weren't enough studs on defense. But Favre racked up 2,588 yards through the air, a school record that still stands, and added another 14 TDs.

"I've never had so much fun coaching as I did working with Brett," Bower said. "He just loves the game, loves to compete. I'm not saying it didn't take some work. We had our moments. He's pretty hard-headed sometimes. I'll bet the coaches at Green Bay could tell you some of the same stories. But I can relate to a quarterback's confidence. At that position, you get a feel for what's going on in the heat of battle, and maybe you think you've got a better feel than the coach. Heck, a lot of times, the quarterback's probably right.

"Basically, we never had any real problem, because Brett was just a great kid who wanted to get better and, for lack of a better way to describe it, he was just a real football player. Miles ahead of everybody else sometimes. He was as intelligent a player as I've ever been around. Football just made sense to him. He understood things right away, which most guys don't.

"We used to work with him separately from the other quarterbacks, because he had so much grasp of things that we'd load him up with more than the others possibly could handle."

Most people familiar with the Southern Mississippi program give Bower a great deal of credit for adding touch to Favre's passing repertoire.

"Brett always had the great arm," Bower said. "God gets credit for that. But the biggest thing we tried to do was establish him as a passer instead of just a thrower. When I first saw him, I'd look at tapes and see that all he knew was to cut it loose. You know, quarterbacks with real strong arms are going to try to force the ball into cracks. They just *are*, because they have so much faith in their ability to squeeze it in there.

"Naturally Brett was like that, but once we changed the passing game a little bit his sophomore year and gave him some options that opened up more of the field, he didn't have to get by with just the arm strength anymore. This is how quickly he picked things up: As just a sophomore, I think he led the nation in lowest percentage of interceptions per attempt (five in 319 throws).

"This is meant as a joke, now, because I have the greatest respect for Mike Holmgren and coaches up in Green Bay, but when Brett had that one really bad year with all those interceptions (24 in 1993), we kidded that he must have learned some bad stuff in the pros, because he never threw those interceptions in college."

There were plenty of thrills around Hattiesburg in 1988,

but among other things, Favre fans remember it for one particular pass.

The Eagles were driving in the final seconds, trying to cover 74 yards and pull out a wild game in which they trailed 42-38 on the road at East Carolina. Favre had been suffering leg cramps all day and had needed first-half relief from Ailrick Young.

But in the midst of the last-gasp march, Favre unloaded a rocket throw that hit streaking wide receiver Alfred Williams right on the hands. The play went for 42 yards to the East Carolina 5-yard line and finished Favre completely. He couldn't move, and Young came back to wrap up the comeback with a game-winning TD throw to Preston Hansford.

Still, the 42-yard bomb set it up, and Williams' reaction after the game became part of Southern Miss football lore. He'd been running as hard as he could, Williams said, when he just suddenly threw up his hands without the luxury of looking back to pick up Favre's fastball in mid-flight.

Williams was asked: How did he know the ball was coming? "I heard it whistling," he said.

Southern Miss partisans still refer to that 45-42 win over East Carolina as "The Whistle Game," in reference to Favre's top-velocity throw and the result it produced. The fact that Brett launched such a bullet with cramps seizing his legs merely adds to the tale.

As exciting and successful as that 10-win year might have been in '88, Favre actually created a couple of his more memorable miracles the next season as Southern Miss was struggling to that 5-6 record.

Two of USM's victories in '89 were storybook jobs, and the most spectacular of all caught Bower right in the middle.

The Eagles opened the season on national TV as 22-point underdogs against Deion Sanders and Florida State — then ranked No. 1 in the nation — at the Gator Bowl in Jacksonville. The previous two seasons, Florida State had pummeled Southern Miss 61-10 and 49-13. But this time, Favre completed 21 of 39 passes for 282 yards and two touchdowns in a 30-26 victory that longtime USM radio voice John Cox called the biggest win in school history.

Actually, Favre pitched for another TD that night, and he'll never forget it.

"The very first play of the game," he said, "I threw a beautiful touchdown pass right to (Sanders). I hit him right in the chest and he danced his way into the end zone."

By the time the evening had run its course, however, all the celebrating was on the other sideline. "Before we went to Jacksonville," Favre said, "people would come up and say, 'Y'all go win this and we'll throw you the biggest party you've ever had when you get back to Hattiesburg.' But when it actually happened, we had a pretty great party ourselves on the field."

For all Favre's heroics, Florida State apparently had staved off the potential upset when Bill Mason kicked a 27-yard field goal to put the Seminoles up 26-24 with 6:57 remaining.

But Southern Miss rallied on its final drive, a 13-play,

58-yard masterpiece that included one serious difference of opinion on the coaching staff.

Once Favre had led the Eagles to a third-and-goal at the Florida State 2-yard line, Hallman called for a running play that would leave the ball in the middle of the field for a potential game-winning field goal.

Upstairs in the coaching booth, Bower wanted something else. "I just figured that FSU would be jamming down in the middle and some kind of rollout pass would be wide open for the touchdown," Bower said. "Normally, I would have agreed with Coach Hallman and gone the conservative way, but Brett gave us the edge. I wouldn't have called a pass with another quarterback, but I felt Brett could pull it off."

Hallman stuck with his run. Bower hollered down for the pass. And Florida State called time out.

Needless to say, Favre voted to throw, and after the coaches finally sorted out their differences, Bower got his call and Southern Miss got its touchdown as Brett ran a naked bootleg around the confused Seminoles and lobbed an easy TD throw to backup tight end Anthony Harris with just 23 seconds remaining.

"All my life I've dreamed of winning a game like this, especially doing it the way we did," Favre said.

Mark McHale has a very special memory of that night. "I can still see Brett and Chris Ryals, this big ol' 300-pound lineman, together in the locker room right after the game," McHale said. "Now Brett loved his linemen — he was just like 'em — but he and Ryals were really something. They were roommates, and Brett used to jump on the guy and get after him somethin' awful. He'd rag him no end.

"Well, after we beat Florida State, there they were, the two of 'em, and their hair was so short they were almost bald, and steam was coming off their heads. They were side by side, right close, both of 'em grinning and exhausted and saying, 'We did it! We did it!' To me, seeing those two boys like that was a picture of college football."

The only down side to that landmark triumph over Florida State is that Southern Mississippi couldn't capitalize on it. Since the Eagles were coming off a 10-2 season, the victory over a No. 1 team produced euphoria in Hattiesburg as it appeared USM might be on the verge of serious national attention.

Unfortunately, the win in Jacksonville was followed by consecutive losses to Mississippi State, Auburn, TCU and Texas A&M. It looked like the dream season was going entirely into the dumper until Southern Miss finally stopped the skid with a 30-21 victory over Tulane.

That left USM's record at 2-4 with a game at Louisville — almost a must-win — up next. And once again the Eagles struggled. In fact, Louisville could have won on Ron Bell's 43-yard field goal try with 13 seconds left and the game tied 10-10.

USM's Vernard Collins blocked the kick, though, and the ball rolled dead on the Southern Miss 21. There was time for two more plays, and now it was time for the Brett Favre legend to reach mythical proportions.

Yes, Favre took a 5-yard sack. But on the next play, he

Favre was prone to improvise long before he got to the pros. Southern
Mississippi's opponents often had to deal with the terror of Brett
on the run while looking to throw the bomb.

threw a 79-yard touchdown pass to Darryl Tillman, wrapping up an impossible 16-10 victory on the last play of the game. Yes, it was a "Hail Mary" call, a tipped ball from one of those everybody-go-long formations. Another receiver, Michael Jackson, batted the ball and Tillman caught it on the dead run to score easily.

"The odds of that happening are unreal," Favre said afterward. "When you go up to the line, you're really thinking it's going to end in a tie. I'm sure that was everybody's feeling."

The result was astonishing, certainly, but possibly an even more remarkable aspect to that game-winning play went almost unnoticed. The tip-and-catch was miraculous, sure, but when Southern Miss coaches went back to look at the game tape, they were even more amazed that Favre had performed an almost superhuman feat just to throw the ball.

"Louisville had this huge All-American defensive lineman named Ted Washington (6-5, 300 pounds)," Thamus Coleman recalled, "and he busted through and had Brett dead. He was all wrapped up, but somehow Brett got away — you'd never know how — and then scrambled way over to his right before he ever let go of the pass. Everything about that play was unbelievable, but Brett Favre is one of the few quarterbacks alive who even could have gotten off a throw, let alone complete it."

For all the individual moments of brilliance and a couple of landmark victories, 1989 had to be considered a disappointment for Southern Miss. Nobody had expected

5-and-6. When the season ended with a 41-27 win over East Carolina, the Eagles and their fans no doubt were thinking about Favre, their genuine Heisman Trophy candidate returning for his senior season. Surely they were saying: "Wait 'til next year."

What nobody knew at the time was that Brett Favre almost wouldn't make it to next year alive.

CHAPTER SIX:
SAY HELLO TO MR. TREE

Until the night of July 14, Brett Favre had only two possible concerns about the upcoming 1990 football season.

Favre had undergone minor elbow surgery the previous spring, but seemed to have healed up fine from that, so problem No. 1 apparently was solved.

The second worry involved continuity on the Southern Mississippi coaching staff. Jeff Bower had been offensive coordinator the previous two years and done so much — installing effective passing schemes and refining Brett's throwing skills — to turn the kid from Hancock County into a potential Heisman Trophy candidate. But Bower left after the '89 season to take a job as assistant head coach at Oklahoma State.

Still, Favre had to be optimistic heading into his senior year. Southern Miss had a decent nucleus of talent surrounding him, and pro scouts already were on the scent, trying to decide how high in the first round Brett might be drafted.

And then came the crash.

Favre was returning early from an outing on Ship Island the evening of the 14th, tooling his 1989 Nissan Maxima over roads in the Diamondhead resort development area that he knew very well. According to a sheriff's investigation conducted later, Brett wasn't speeding and there was no indication that he was impaired by alcohol.

The best Favre can recollect about the events of that night, he was heading along Kapalama Drive sometime around mid-evening — less than a mile from his parents' home in Fenton — when he met an oncoming car whose driver didn't dim his lights. But Favre still can't remember exactly what happened after that.

"I think it basically blinded him so he went off on the side of the road, hit the shoulder and went a little bit out of control there," said Favre's dad Irvin. "He jerked back and that's when he lost control. Then he left the road, went up and hit a tree in a little wooded area there."

Favre probably was lucky to survive. His Maxima was totaled. But Brett was rushed to Memorial Hospital in Gulfport and placed in intensive care with internal injuries that originally were diagnosed as a bruised liver, minor cuts and scrapes and a concussion.

Dr. Jare Barkley, Favre's physician, seemed guardedly optimistic that his patient wouldn't suffer any permanent effects from the wreck. "We got a CAT scan of his brain and there's no evidence of any hematoma, blood clot or

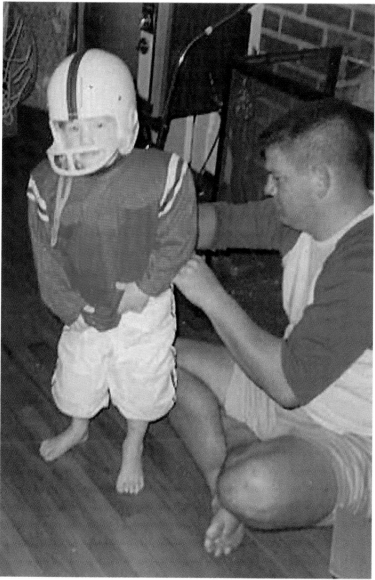

Coach Irvin Favre suits up young Brett in a
football uniform — the first of many to come.

photo by Tim Isbell, The Sun Herald

Brett Favre changed the football landscape at the University of
Southern Mississippi, befuddling Florida State and a host of
other big-time opponents during his four years as starter.

photo by Tim Isbell, The Sun Herald

Draft day 1991 was exciting for Brett and his pals. Atlanta
grabbed the Southern Miss quarterback with the 33rd overall
selection, but it turned out his future was in Green Bay.

Once just a scrambler struggling to learn a complicated pro offense,
Favre has became a deadly weapon for the Packers by
hanging in the pocket to deliver his bombs.

photo by Tim Isbell, The Sun Herald

Brett has never gotten far from his roots. In 1994, he nominated his fourth-grade teacher at Hancock North Central Elementary School, Bill Ray Dedeaux (to Brett's right) as the NFL's "Teacher of the Month." (above)

By the time the Packers celebrated their 75th anniversary in 1993 – note the shoulder patch – Favre had become an established pro star. (right)

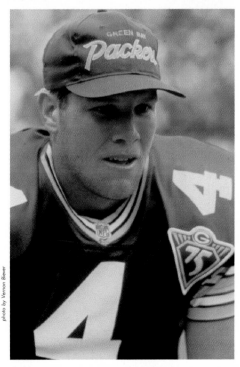

photo by Vernon Biever

A familiar sight at Lambeau Field: Brett celebrates another touchdown throw with his arms flung skyward. (left)

There's plenty to think about for the leader of a championship NFL team. Brett takes time to sit back and reflect on other things to accomplish. (below)

photo by Vernon Biever

photo by Vernon Biever

photo by Vernon Biever

Favre and Packers' coach Mike Holmgren had some difficult moments early in their relationship, but now they're right on the same page.

photo by John Fitzhugh, The Sun Herald

The entire Favre clan: Irvin and Bonita stand behind their brood — from the left, Scott, Brett, Jeff and Brandi. That's Duke down in front.

photo by Vernon Biever

photo by Vernon Biever

Favre went through some tough times during the 1996 off-season, conceding that he was addicted to painkillers and admitting himself for six weeks of treatment. But the Packers' star emerged confident that good times were ahead. At the press conference following his rehab stint, Brett joked with coach Mike Holmgren. Just four days earlier (bottom), Brett married his longtime sweetheart, Deanna Tynes. Both mothers posed with the happy couple: Ann Tynes on the left and Bonita Favre next to Brett.

anything like that," Barkley said. There was a small hematoma in the liver, but Barkley indicated he expected it to dissolve on its own.

"At first, we were concerned that it was something much worse," said Bonita Favre, Brett's mother. "It was a scary day right after the crash. People who saw the car wrapped around that tree couldn't believe Brett got out alive, and just hearing that alone was enough to make you shiver."

Within a couple of days of the accident, however, all the initial panic had turned to thoughts of football. The crash happened on a Saturday night, and by the following Tuesday, Favre was briefly up and walking — and talking about when he could rejoin his Southern Miss teammates, who were scheduled to begin practice Aug. 13.

"I'll be back," Favre said with his customary bravado. "I'm bruised up and sore, but I don't have any broken bones (one early report suggested he had busted his left arm). So I'll be ready for the first game.

"Sunday and Monday, I was much sorer than I am today. Right now, when I'm still, there isn't much pain. When I try to move, especially to my right, it's still pretty painful. It's just a matter of getting over the soreness and getting back in shape. I might miss a week or two of practice, but I should be OK pretty soon."

That announcement caused immense relief for Southern Miss fans, who had been flooding the hospital switchboard with calls. But as it turned out, neither Brett nor his doctors realized that the damage inside was far more severe than they thought.

Favre was released from Memorial on July 22, and the medical staff's only concern seemed to be that their patient, a noted overachiever, might get carried away rushing his rehabilitation. "From what I've heard, he's a tough kid and that could help his recovery," Barkley said, "but at the same time, pain is the body telling you, 'Don't do that.' His tolerance for pain could be either a plus or a minus. He shouldn't be so tough that he ignores pain."

Given Favre's state of mind right then, Barkley's caution appeared justified. "They're sending me a playbook this week," Brett said, "so I'll start studying the plays, getting ready."

As it turned out, however, Favre was a long, long way from being healthy and less than a month later, he was back in the hospital for abdominal surgery.

"After I got out of the hospital in Gulfport, I had soreness in my stomach muscles," Favre said. "It seemed like I'd just gotten bruised by the seat belt in the accident. But the doctors thought the thing would loosen up and the soreness would go away. Instead, I kept feeling pain and finally it started to get worse."

By that time, Brett was in Hattiesburg, so he was admitted to Forrest General Hospital for further evaluation. At Forrest, Dr. George McGee found that the stomach injury had caused an intestinal blockage, which constricted the flow of blood in the small intestine.

Thus on Aug. 8, McGee performed an hour-and-a-half operation to remove about a 30-inch portion of Brett's small intestine. The prognosis, however, was excellent. In a press conference that remains the largest ever held at Forrest, McGee explained to reporters that because doctors had been able to make a fairly small incision, Favre's time for full recovery would be relatively short.

McGee estimated that Brett could begin workouts in three to five weeks and "full, unrestricted activity" in five or six weeks. At that rehabilitation pace, it appeared the earliest Favre possibly could rejoin the team would be in time for USM's third game, Sept. 15 against Georgia.

"It's good to know at this point where we and Brett are headed," Eagles coach Curley Hallman said. "At this particular point, things certainly look brighter than they have in recent days.

"It's been an extremely tough time for Brett — elbow surgery in the spring, the recent wreck and complications from that. Knowing Brett, I'm sure he'll do everything possible to effect an early and complete rehabilitation."

But for the first time since the accident, even the normally irrepressible Favre admitted he was having some doubts. Southern Miss assistant coach Mark McHale visited Brett at Forrest and found the quarterback and his mother both looking glum.

"Bonita told me, 'This really doesn't look good,' " McHale said. "I came right back and told her, 'Bonita, I'm disappointed in you. This isn't the time to quit fighting.'

"I set up a board right there in the hospital room and started diagramming some football stuff, and it was like a light went on in the room. Brett sat right up in bed, his eyes got bright again, and you could tell just thinking about getting back on the field picked up his spirits.

"I knew he'd be back. I just never imagined he'd come back when he did or what he'd do. But I should have known. That kid can do anything he sets his mind to do."

Looking back, Favre's accident in mid-July had far more long-term effects than simply delaying his appearance at quarterback for Southern Miss at the start of the 1990 season.

For one thing, however much a longshot he might have been — stuck down in the media backwater of Hatties-burg — the surgery definitely knocked out any shot Brett had as a serious contender for the Heisman. Southern Miss, even without much national exposure and no conference affiliation at that point, had turned out some tremendous NFL talents — punter Ray Guy is in the Hall of Fame — and the school had geared up a serious Heisman campaign for Brett's senior season.

So that was out.

And then there was the matter of pro football, surely Favre's next destination following the 1990 season. Who knew when he'd be able to play? And even if he did get back under center that year, naturally he'd be weak and underweight — not to mention months late putting in normal game preparation.

As for all the NFL scouts who were drooling over Brett during his junior year, they became an obvious question mark. Teams are notoriously reluctant to take many chances on players with shaky medical histories, and that would especially be true in the case of a possible No. 1 draft choice.

"By the time I'd finished my junior year, I really had a pretty good idea of how I stacked up against other quarterbacks, including some pretty good ones," Favre said. "I could see that I had a chance to play in the pros, and that's every player's dream. So sure, after the accident I wondered what would happen to my dream."

Then finally, from a perspective that only came into focus six years later, you wonder how much the pain medication Brett received following the accident and subsequent surgery contributed to the addiction that dropped him to rock bottom in 1996.

"Bonita and I have always felt that the problem (with Vicodin) probably went all the way back to the car crash," Irvin Favre said. "That's been our belief from the beginning. Brett wasn't a kid who was bothered by a little hurt. He wasn't the type to be grabbing a painkiller just for a twisted ankle or something like that. We really feel that it took something major — like the accident — to get that stuff in his system in the first place."

Irvin Favre feels strongly that his son's ultimate revelation that the painkillers had hooked him came from a combination of factors. "Starting with the accident and some of the injuries he had when he got to the pros," Irvin said, "you add it up and it can get to you. I'm not blaming anybody in particular, but I did worry — even before Brett went in for treatment — that these pain pills get passed around like candy.

"I'm not saying I'm against players being treated for pain. It's a tough game and guys get hurt. And this isn't just about Green Bay. I'm sure they try to follow the rules. But I've been a coach most of my life and I've been around a lot of players who were injured one way or another. I just feel like pain medication should be much more controlled than it is.

"Our son happened to be the one to come forward and tell everyone what was going on with him, and that he was getting help. But there are plenty of other players with the same problem, and I believe part of it is that sometimes these painkillers are handed out like M&Ms.

"They're out there if you want 'em, whether it's from doctors or other players or whoever, and I hope Brett's case shows everybody how dangerous that is."

Back in 1990, though, future bouts with pharmaceuticals were the least of Brett Favre's worries. More than anything, he wanted to get back on the football field at Southern Miss. And so typically, he threw himself into getting well.

And was immediately frustrated.

"I remember Brett being really discouraged around the time of fall practice," USM staff member Thamus Coleman said. "Four or five days before our first game against Delta State, Brett didn't look like he'd be able to play for months. He was weak and he didn't have anything like his normal velocity on the football.

"I think there was discussion about a possible redshirt season, because Brett had played as a true freshman, so he would have had another year of eligibility if he sat out. But

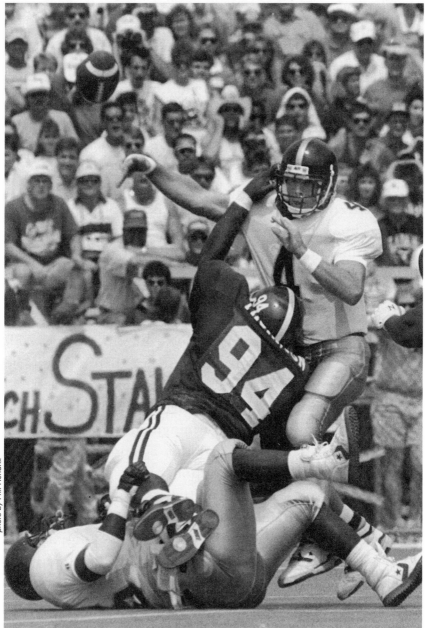

photo by Phil Hendrix

The ultimate tribute to Brett's toughness and leadership abilities:
the upset of Alabama barely two months after his car accident.

you know Brett. The thought of sitting out would just about kill him."

Favre watched from the sideline as Southern Miss opened with a lackluster 12-0 victory over toothless Delta State, but the next two games on the schedule were Alabama and Georgia. These were the sort of big-dog teams that Brett loved to face, always looking to prove himself against impossible odds.

And so it was time for another Brett Favre miracle.

"The week of the Alabama game, Brett made it clear he wanted to play if the doctors would let him," Coleman said. "I know the doctor called Irvin and talked to him about it. Finally, they made the decision that it would be up to the coaches, because Brett was medically OK. He wasn't going to tear anything loose, in other words, so it wouldn't hurt him to play. It's just that there's no way he was physically ready for the likes of Alabama."

But ready or not, Favre convinced Hallman and the staff that he could play in Birmingham.

Powerful Alabama (24-3 all-time against Southern Miss) would be a frightening opponent for a half-strength quarterback under any circumstances. But just to make the task even more daunting, the Tide would be playing their first game under new head coach Gene Stallings, a wildly popular protégé of the late Bear Bryant who figured to have his team at fever pitch for his coming-out party.

Hallman wavered on his quarterback decision until the morning of the game, but at last he let emotion win out and chose Favre to start ahead of freshman John Whitcomb, who had played the week before against Delta State.

"There was no way Brett was in any kind of condition to make a great impact throwing the ball or doing the things he usually did," recalled USM sports information director Regiel Napier, "but the difference in the game was just the fact that Brett was on the field. The inspiration he brought to it. It was like he lifted the whole team up a foot off the ground and the rest of guys said, 'If Brett's out here, we can do this.' "

And they did, notching a remarkable 27-24 upset when Jim Taylor launched a 52-yard field goal — into the wind — with 3:35 left to play.

"It was the kind of game you remember all your life," Coleman said. "You're playing one of the most famous programs in the country, at their place, in Stallings' first game. It's like you're being fed to the lions. And then somehow Brett goes out there and everybody plays better football than they even know how. Our defense gave up a bunch of yards (442), but they kept coming up with big plays and turnovers to keep us in it.

"What a thrill that was for those kids at the end. I thought to myself: I want to hold onto this feeling for a long time, because days like this don't come around that often."

Favre completed just 9 of 17 passes for 125 yards, but he stood his ground against the furious 'Bama defense and connected on some key throws when the game was hanging in the balance. Naturally, Brett was the trigger man on the final drive that led to Taylor's winning kick.

"I didn't feel any pain out there," Favre said afterward, "but I got really tired."

In fact, Brett couldn't quite go the distance no matter how pumped up he was to play. Whitcomb worked a few series at quarterback just to give Favre a breather and keep him upright for the fourth quarter.

The victory over Alabama did more than re-establish Favre's reputation as a magic man. It helped launch Southern Miss to an 8-3 regular season during which Favre was reasonably effective, but still merely a shadow of himself.

"What he couldn't do with his arm that year, he did with his leadership," Coleman said. "There were times when I know the rest of the guys just said, 'We can't let Brett down.' That's the effect he had."

Ten games into the '90 season, Southern Miss was 7-3 and — as an independent — desperately needed one more quality victory to jump into the postseason bowl picture. And the last test of the year was a road game at 15th-ranked Auburn.

Even the most faithful USM fan couldn't dream of defeating Alabama and Auburn in the same season. That sounded like fantasy, but once again, with Favre around, the impossible happens more often than logic dictates.

And this time, with nearly a full season of recovery behind him, Brett's arm was back near cannon strength.

As 85,214 at Jordan-Hare Stadium watched in disbelief, Favre took over the game after Auburn had bullied its way to a 12-0 lead with just a quarter to play. That margin could

University of Southern Mississippi
Head Coach Jeff Bower

have been bigger, but the USM defense forced Auburn to settle for four field goals on first-half drives that could have blown the game open.

So given an opportunity to win the thing (he'd already led three comeback victories that year), Favre promptly went out and did it again.

First off, he closed the gap to 12-7 with a 10-yard TD strike to Michael Jackson with 8:04 remaining, thus finishing a 69-yard drive that represented the Eagles' last reasonable chance to stay in the game.

And then, after Tony Smith's 14-yard punt return put Southern Miss back in business at the Auburn 42 with time running out, Favre applied the hammer. Brett engineered one of his patented desperation drives, and capped it with a perfect 10-yard touchdown throw to Anthony Harris just 46 ticks from the end.

Southern Mississippi 13, Auburn 12.

"I had somebody playing me man-to-man," Harris said. "Brett did a great job of staying with me and waiting until he thought I was open. He put the ball right in there and I watched it all the way in."

By the way, if that Favre-Harris combination rings a bell, it should. Harris, a tight end who rarely figured in the Eagles' passing game, also caught the winning TD pass with 23 seconds left in that 30-26 upset of Florida State the previous year.

Favre, who had his best day of the year against Auburn with 24 completions in 40 attempts for 207 yards and those two huge touchdowns, called the triumph the most satisfying of his life.

"It has to be the biggest win I've ever been associated with," Brett said. "They get bigger every time. We've beaten two of the top teams in the country. Maybe Alabama is struggling a little bit and Auburn lost a big one last week (to Florida), but we had to play them at their places both times in front of sellout crowds."

Curley Hallman hailed the victory as a major turning point for the Southern Mississippi program. "Like I told Pat (Auburn coach Pat Dye) after the game, to beat a Pat Dye team and Auburn is a great honor," Hallman said. "It's one of those big moments in life. This puts us further around the turn. It's a huge step."

Ironically, Hallman was right about it being a big moment in *his* life. Even as Southern Miss was accepting a bid to play North Carolina State in the All American Bowl in Birmingham, Hallman resigned to take the coaching job at Louisiana State.

And as if that turn of events wasn't crazy enough for a year that started with the Top Gun Favre surviving a car accident, Southern Miss immediately lured Jeff Bower back from Oklahoma State as its next head coach.

Bower returned in time to coach Favre one last time in the bowl game. "Boy, I just got in there and told Brett first thing, 'We're opening up and going for it all,' " Bower said. "If I was only going to have him for one more game, I made up my mind we'd be throwing the football everywhere but into the press box. No use leaving anything in the sack.

"Truthfully, it was really tough on the kids in the program to lose their coach and have to work with a new staff just before a bowl game, and I knew our only chance was if Brett went wild."

It almost turned out that way. Favre had a big day in the All American Bowl, but this time the weary Southern Miss defense couldn't hold the fort and North Carolina State hung on to win 31-27.

So how can you sum up Brett Favre's senior season at Southern Miss?

No Heisman Trophy, obviously. Not particularly gaudy numbers — only 1,572 yards passing and seven touchdowns after 45 TDs his first three years. An untimely coaching change between the end of the season and a bowl game. Yet on the flip side, there were those monumental upsets at Alabama and Auburn, victories that have become legendary around Hattiesburg.

"It was a weird year all around," Favre said. "I really wasn't myself physically until the very end. By the time we played Auburn and North Carolina State, I had my strength back and we could do some of the things we'd done before. But early in the year, maybe I should have been resting in my room.

"Still, we went 8-4 and got the bowl invitation, we whipped 'Bama and Auburn and did it in the fourth quarter both times with the crowd just screaming at us. So from a team standpoint, (1990) had to be considered a good year, and football is a team game.

"The quarterback's job is to win, not throw for a million yards, and we had quite a few big wins. It was a strange year, but I think for Southern Miss football, it was a good one — and I know it was awfully exciting."

And as for his NFL aspirations?

Bower was positive. "I had no doubt that Brett would make it in pro football," he said. "I've been fortunate to be around some really good ones, and by far, he was the best. There were no limits to what you could do with him.

"He's got what it takes. Nothing intimidates him at all. The bigger the game, the better he is. He gives you a chance every time you take the field. He was an equalizer for us. He made everybody around him better.

"No, I wasn't worried about him being a success in the NFL at all. They haven't made a level of football where Brett Favre isn't going to be a star."

Favre conceded, though, that after all he'd been through, he wasn't quite so sure what kind of chance he'd get in the pros. He'd had elbow surgery, after all, and then the mess after the car accident.

"I didn't know what to think," he said. "I guess all I could hope was that the scouts would go by what I could do when I was healthy instead of worrying about how I looked when I wasn't. I had to trust that somebody in the NFL would look at my sophomore and junior years, and then maybe at the end of the last year, and make their judgment on that.

"I still believed by then that I could make it big in the NFL. I had to wait and see if somebody in the league agreed with me."

And yes, somebody did.

CHAPTER SEVEN:
STAY CLOSE TO THE TOILET

There are less than a hundred thousand residents in Green Bay, but surely a half-million people will tell you they were in Lambeau Field that afternoon when Brett Favre threw his first miracle touchdown pass in the NFL.

To listen to the Packer faithful, that 24-23 victory over Cincinnati on the third weekend of the 1992 season perhaps ranks second only to the Ice Bowl of '67 in real and imagined attendance.

Favre's 35-yard bullet to Kittrick Taylor with 19 seconds remaining after the Mississippi Kid came off the bench to replace injured starter Don Majkowski?

"I have to admit I can see why so many people remember it," said former Packer quarterback and radio commentator Lynn Dickey. "I mean, even for fans watching on TV, it must have *felt* like they were there at the stadium because it was the kind of play that takes your breath away.

"As a quarterback myself, I was impressed with that

whole last drive, when Brett — who'd never been in that situation as a pro — just seemed to be telling the guys, 'Jump on my back and we're gonna win.'

"But that throw to Taylor...I mean, Brett whipped that thing down the sideline on a rope. It was the kind that makes you go, 'Whoa! What have we got here?' That's the sort of thing that leaves the defensive backs looking at each other and saying, "What was that? How'd he do that?' "

Favre himself admitted wondering exactly what he'd accomplished. "That last ball," he said, "I was scared I was going to throw it halfway up into the stands. I just closed my eyes and waited for the cheering."

Actually, Favre has been hearing thunderous applause most of the time since then.

Not that there haven't been some hiccups: 24 interceptions along with a few boos in 1993, a brief Mark Brunell-for-quarterback whispering campaign midway through '94 and, of course, the much-publicized bout with painkiller addiction following Brett's MVP season in 1995.

Favre survived the first couple of rough spots with help and assurance from coach Mike Holmgren and quarterback coach Steve Mariucci. "I had to tell him straight out that he was the guy," Holmgren said. "I didn't want him to worry about looking over his shoulder. I let him know that he and I were joined at the hip. I more or less said, 'Brett, if you go in the dumper, I'm going in with you.' "

Needless to say, there hasn't been a dumper around any corners so far. Yes, Favre needs to defeat the painkiller demons that knocked his life out of whack and otherwise stay relatively healthy over the next few years. But if those two things occur, the marriage between Brett Favre and the Green Bay Packers can only be a spectacular success.

The most amazing part of the story, though, might be how Favre and the Pack got hitched in the first place.

Flash back to Brett's senior year at Southern Mississippi: Remember, he was recovering most of that year from serious abdominal surgery which had left him 20 pounds underweight. He really couldn't deliver the football with his customary velocity until the last two or three games of that 1990 season.

Meantime, the NFL scouts came calling as they do on most major campuses every fall. And one of the visitors to Hattiesburg that year was the New York Jets' director of player personnel, Ron Wolf.

Southern Miss had plenty of talent to evaluate — the Eagles had three players taken in the subsequent draft — and so Wolf went through his usual routine, which included long, solitary sessions in a dark room watching hours of tape.

"I remember being intrigued by Brett, because the coaches loved him and everybody talked about the way he carried himself, the way he was such a winner," Wolf said. "But then I got in there with those tapes, which were games from his senior season, and it just wasn't anything really special. You could see he could play, but this was a guy who had been discussed as a first-round pick, and with somebody like that, you're looking for him to jump right off the screen at you."

And that might have been the end of it: Wolf would have written up Favre as a potential project and moved along to the next place. Except that Wolf's day was done early, and he had some time to kill.

"I hope the people down there aren't offended by this," Wolf said, "but there isn't all that much to do spending a spare afternoon in Hattiesburg. So I had some time, and Thamus Coleman, the football staff guy there in charge of working with pro scouts, suggested maybe I ought to look at some tapes from Brett's *junior* year. Before the car accident.

"So I said, 'What the heck?' Sure, let's do it."

Coleman recalled it well. He felt that Wolf and other pro scouts who were seeing tape of Brett from early in the '90 season weren't watching the real McCoy. The boy had been so weak, playing mostly on guts and guile, until his strength started coming back near the end of the season.

"I'd heard of Ron Wolf, of course," Coleman said, "but I'd never met him until he came to Hattiesburg that day. I kind of knew what he was thinking after he watched the first set of tapes and I told him he wasn't really seeing Brett Favre. I told him if he saw just one game, Memphis State, from the season before, he might have a different opinion."

Wolf watched, and he *did* have a different opinion. He became convinced that Favre might be the steal of the draft because of the preseason surgery he'd had that previous summer.

Meanwhile, Brett finished out the year throwing the ball about as well as he ever had, and prepared for a couple of all-star games that would serve as audition for pro scouts. He was scheduled to play in the Senior Bowl in Mobile, then the East-West Shrine Classic out at Stanford.

The Senior Bowl makes no pretense of being a showcase for the NFL. Pro coaches handle both squads — which are called the AFC and NFC — and scouts dot the stadium. Favre's coach was Jim Mora of the New Orleans Saints, everyone's favorite team back home in southern Mississippi, and Mora named Brett as a starter.

In the week prior to the game, Favre was interviewed by dozens of pro scouts and coaches. Unless they were kidding him, Brett decided, just about everyone projected him as a first- or second-round pick.

"But you can never tell," he said. "I could end up going in the fifth. It all depends on who wants a quarterback and what kind of quarterback they want. But I would be disappointed if I went as late as the fifth round. I guess it would mean that I'm not as good as the rest of the guys and I feel like I am."

Curiously, for someone with the confidence Favre usually projects, he admitted to a case of nerves before the Senior Bowl. "The first of the week, when I came in, I said, 'Once the game gets here, it's going to be no big deal.' But now I'm kind of jumpy."

As it turned out, Brett had reason to be apprehensive. The Senior Bowl was a disaster.

Working against a brutal rush and dealing with bad footing at Ladd Stadium, Favre completed a paltry 7 of 15 passes for 62 yards. Normally elusive in the pocket, he was sacked three times and lost a fumble. After one bruising hit in the third quarter, he began limping.

Bottom line: Brett was the least impressive quarterback in the game. By contrast, teammate Dan McGwire of San Diego State hit 11 of 23 throws for 165 yards and two touchdowns in a 38-28 loss.

"Hell, I got killed," Favre said afterward. "What I need is a cold beer. That's what I need. It wasn't fun. I didn't enjoy it. I'm glad I came, but I'm coming away with a lot of bruises.

"All (an all-star game) is, is a game of pitch and catch. I didn't get the protection that some of the other guys got, though. For me, it was more a game of getting killed than pitch and catch."

In the week leading up to the Senior Bowl, Favre recalled getting special attention in conversations with people from the Broncos, Washington, Cleveland, the Jets (remember Ron Wolf?), the Giants, the Bills and Houston. In fact, he'd had dinner on Thursday night with Oilers general manager Mike Holovak.

Who knew what any of them thought after the game?

The East-West game out in California was scheduled just one week after the Senior Bowl, on Jan. 26. For that reason, not too many players want to come right back and put their goods on the line with such a short week of preparation. Especially quarterbacks, who have to learn some kind of offense — no matter how simple the coaches try to make it.

Favre would have played in both games no matter what,

just because he loves to strap it on, but after the Senior Bowl fiasco, his appearance in California took on added importance.

And what was it his old coordinator at Southern Miss, Jeff Bower, said over and over? "The bigger the game, the better Brett's going to play."

Bower knew his man: Despite the short week of practice, Favre was a star at Stanford, completing 15 of 26 passes for 218 yards, throwing a 54-yard bomb to Lamonde Russell of Alabama for one touchdown and using a nifty pump fake to set up a 7-yard TD run of his own. Brett was named co-offensive player of the game.

And Ron Wolf was there.

"All I could think of," Wolf said, "is that about once a generation, a quarterback comes along who has this particular quality, and that's the ability to make it seem as though the whole field is tilting one way whenever he's out there. That's what it was like at the East-West game. Brett just completely dominating the day.

"He had so many things you're looking for at the quarterback position. He seemed to be a natural leader, a win-at-all-costs player. He had great skill and ability. It was just a matter of harnessing that talent. I thought he would be an outstanding player.

"I walked out of there after the East-West game and told our people, 'Brett Favre is the best college quarterback in the country. We've got to get him.' "

By the time of the NFL draft in April, Wolf had convinced his general manager, the late Dick Steinberg, that Favre could be a potential franchise quarterback. Unfortunately for the Jets — but fortuitously for the Packers, who weren't even in the picture at that point — New York didn't have a first-round selection in the '91 draft.

"We had (Favre) No. 2 on our entire draft board," Wolf said. "Dick Steinberg was trying to work a deal with somebody to move up so we could take him with our first pick. We weren't able to move up, though, but for awhile, it seemed that we might be able to get him anyway."

Almost.

The Jets, selecting 34th, had to sweat out just one more call when Atlanta snatched Favre in the second round with the 33rd overall choice. The Jets settled for Louisville quarterback Browning Nagle and Wolf naturally was disappointed, but it seemed like a logical move for the Falcons, who had nobody in the wings to develop behind starting quarterback Chris Miller.

Initally, Favre was thrilled with the draft. He was staying in Dixie, getting to face the hometown hero Saints twice a year in the NFC West and apparently being groomed — under run-and-shoot quarterback guru June Jones — as a future pro star.

But then came the stunner: Just before the '91 season began, Atlanta traded for well-traveled veteran Billy Joe Tolliver and immediately installed him as Miller's backup. Favre was relegated to clipboard duty, or worse, at No. 3.

"When I got there," Brett said, "it looked like I'd be the backup, which was fine because as the backup I felt that I'd have a chance to play at some point during the season. But then they traded for Billy Joe.

"I walked in one day and boom, I'm third-string. No explanation. No discussion. That just killed me. I knew that I wouldn't have any chance to play, and for somebody who had never sat on the bench his whole life, that was hard to accept."

And Brett will be the first to admit he didn't handle the situation well at all. He hurled himself into Atlanta's well-known nightclub scene and when he wasn't quaffing several beers, he must have been at the dinner table.

"All he did was drink beer and eat chicken wings for a year," said Jerry Glanville, then the Falcons' unconventional and outspoken coach and now a TV broadcaster. "He looked like the Pillsbury doughboy."

"I just said, 'The hell with it,' " Favre admitted. "I went out every night, gained weight and was out of shape. I didn't study, I didn't care. I'd show up just in time for the meetings and I'd be out of there the second the meetings were over."

Or, to hear Glanville tell it, often the kid from Mississippi didn't bother with meetings at all.

"He's the only guy I've ever coached in 31 years who missed the team picture," Glanville said. "That didn't sit too good with me. With Brett, I'd put numbers on the board for his excuses. I used to tell him not to make up excuses; just give me a number. I didn't want to listen to it. With the picture, I think it was a terrible accident, but nobody died.

Not a scratch on him. The only blood I saw was in his eyes."

Atlanta players apparently recognized the possible greatness in Brett's arm, but they also realized he'd gone in the tank once he'd been relegated to the last seat on the bench.

"He didn't have a whole lot of attentiveness," Falcons special teams player Elbert Shelley said. "I think he was kind of lackadaisical at times. Whether he got into that because he wasn't playing, that's a matter of opinion. I thought he was a good quarterback."

Falcon linebacker Jessie Tuggle told stories of Favre, used as quarterback on the scout team, forcing powerhouse throws into near-impossible coverage, perhaps just for the hell of it. But Tuggle's recollection was that Favre did it all with such arm strength and personal cockiness that a lot of his teammates thought he might someday be a star.

Back in Hattiesburg that fall, Bower winced at Favre's misery, but the coach wasn't entirely surprised.

"I think his experience in Atlanta was a wake-up call," Bower said. "Here's a guy who had probably everything come to him pretty easily. You jump up another level, and you assume it's going to happen like it always has.

"Knowing how competitive Brett is, it got his attention. In hindsight, it's probably good that it happened."

Ironically, there actually were a few highlights to Favre's lost year in Atlanta. He had some decent moments in the preseason, and though he threw just five passes in the regular season and missed them all, the Falcons went 10-

6, made the playoffs and won their first-round game in New Orleans, of all places. Favre joked that although he earned a playoff check, half the money went for tickets since all his family and friends wanted to see the Saints and Falcons at the Superdome.

In retrospect, it seemed a foregone conclusion — given Glanville's displeasure and Favre's apparent lack of commitment — that Brett would be shipped out of town before sundown as soon as the season ended. But that wasn't the case. In fact, he was in for yet another shock when the trade actually happened.

"I talked to June Jones (after the Tolliver trade) and said, 'What's the deal?' " Favre recalled. "He said they brought Billy in for insurance purposes, for experience and that they just wanted to give me a year to learn and progress. They didn't want to put me in too many situations, as young as I was.

"June said they planned to keep me around for a long time. I asked him about going to play overseas in the World League, and he said, 'Well, I got news for you. We're not going to let you play in it.' That kind of made me feel good that they cared enough about me to think that I'm going to be their man, so they didn't want me playing over there.

"After we lost to Washington (in the playoffs), we had a meeting and June told me, 'You're protected (from Plan B free agency), and we're not getting rid of you.' So that was a good sign."

Also a false one.

Now that Favre has become the league's MVP, everyone

involved with his ultimate departure from Atlanta has a slightly different version of whose decision it was to move him. General manager Ken Herock claimed Glanville had given up on Brett and wanted him gone, but Glanville has said he was sick when he heard the news he'd been traded — which he insisted came as a complete surprise.

"(Favre) was not Jerry Glanville's favorite," Herock said. "He didn't want me to draft him. He wouldn't give the kid a break. Every time I came back from a scouting trip, Jerry was critical of him in all areas. He was overweight, he wasn't working hard, he wasn't accurate, he wasn't dedicated. It was like I drafted the worst guy in professional football.

"Realistically, if your coach is down on a guy like that, you have to move him. But with Brett Favre, you can definitely say I did it with reluctance."

Ah yes, the trade.

That brings the story back to Ron Wolf, who left the Jets to become general manager of the Packers in November of '91.

Wolf had conceded many times that, with all he had on his plate taking over the football operations in Green Bay — his first priority was firing coach Lindy Infante and replacing him with Mike Holmgren — he hadn't been paying particular attention to how Favre was behaving in Atlanta. All Wolf remembered was what he'd seen on tape and in that East-West Shrine game. He still believed Favre could be one of the league's next great quarterbacks.

"What's the saying? The Lord takes care of the dumb

STAY CLOSE TO THE TOILET

or whatever?" Wolf said. "That was me. I didn't know about any of that stuff (in Atlanta)."

Actually, while he might not have been conducting bed-checks on Favre in Atlanta, Wolf was sandbagging a little when he suggested he was keeping up with Favre. The Packers' first game after Wolf was named GM — Dec. 1, 1991 — happened to be against Atlanta, and Wolf paced the sidelines beforehand to watch Brett throw the ball in warm-ups. And he was still impressed.

Thus Wolf got busy reminding the Packers' executive committee — most still wide-eyed over his sudden dismissal of Infante — that he'd braced them for a complete overhaul and that when he saw a player who could help the franchise, he planned to act quickly.

And Wolf was sure Brett Favre could be the savior in Green Bay.

So, early in 1992, Wolf began negotiating with the Falcons, who seemed intent on robbing him. When the deal was announced, in fact, most NFL observers thought that's exactly what had happened. The Packers got Favre, a second-round pick who had made no impact and was running third-string, for a first-round choice (No. 17).

Even Favre couldn't believe it.

"It looked like a good deal for Atlanta," he said. "Who would have known it would work out the way it did."

But Wolf's reasoning was sound: He understood Green Bay needed to groom a quarterback to replace Majkowski (whom the Packers knew had a bum arm) sooner or later, and that picking in the 17th spot, he couldn't see that they

Brett Favre getting ready for action in his favorite place to play,
Green Bay's historic Lambeau Field.

could get anyone who matched Favre's upside. And the Packers had a first-rounder to spend: They retained the fifth overall selection.

Still, the furor in Green Bay...

"When the deal was made, I had a lot of phone calls," Wolf said. "Most of them weren't positive. But I've always believed that you have to go with what you believe in, not what's popular. From the very start, I liked what I saw in Brett. I kept thinking back to that day in Hattiesburg, and the sheer chance that Thamus Coleman suggested I look at some more tape. But after that, I never doubted that Brett was the player we needed.

"But basically, I was staking my whole career on Brett. It was really the first move I made here as GM. I caught the devil for it. If it hadn't worked out..."

For his part, Holmgren backed Wolf on the trade from Day One. At the press conference announcing Favre's acquisition, Holmgren — himself a rookie head coach without a single game under his belt — told the media: "When you get a chance to get a quarterback that you think is a great one, you do it. So that's what we did."

Was Holmgren saying, having never seen Favre in an NFL game, that he was getting a great one?

"I think he can be," Holmgren replied. "He's young and he has everything I look for to play the position. What separates the great ones from the good ones is how hard they work. But he's got all the stuff."

Wisconsin-area reporters also got their first taste of Irvin Favre once the trade was completed. No doubt that was an eye-opener.

"I remember the Packers tradition, ever since I was a young-un," Irvin said. "The fans there want to win badly. So does Brett. He's the most hard-headed of my sons. He's mean. He's raw-boned. He's a battler."

To illustrate his boy's personality, Irvin recounted a phone call in which June Jones — by then Favre's good friend — tried to explain how the Falcons could let him go. Irvin said the call ended with Brett telling his pal, "Hey June, I think we play y'all next year. I think if I'm playing, we're going to kick your butts."

Irvin Favre also divulged the information that the Packers weren't the only bidders trying to pry Brett loose from Atlanta. Irvin's conversations with Falcons executives led him to believe that at least two other teams (Denver and Kansas City) were interested, but that the asking price was high. After all, Atlanta had protected Brett in Plan B.

"What the Falcons told me was the Packers made the best final offer," Irvin said. "Green Bay really wanted Brett."

June Jones understood why.

"Ron Wolf is very capable and very aware," Jones said after losing his protégé to the Packers. "He had a pretty good feel in this trade. Brett's a competitor and he's got a big arm. The Packers knew what they were getting when they traded for him. If you wait until the 17th pick, well, you just never know.

"In time, I think it will prove out to be a good choice for the Packers."

Jones also added that Favre would benefit from working with Holmgren. "Mike did such a great job at San Francisco

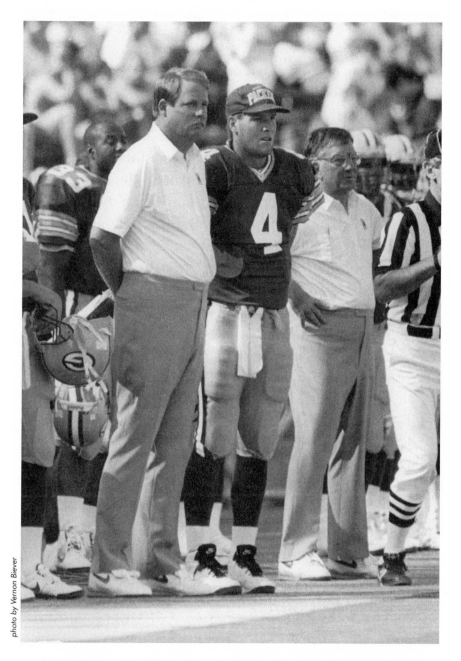

The Packer trigger men watch from the sidelines: Mike Holmgren (left) and Favre.

of taking Steve Bono out of obscurity and, by the end of the season, making him look like Joe Montana," Jones said. "I think he could do the same for Brett."

As the 1995 season wound down, with Favre en route to an MVP and leading the Packers to the NFC championship game, it was easy to find ironies all over the lot: Green Bay defeated Atlanta — under head coach June Jones — in the first round of the playoffs; Glanville, in the TV booth, spun yarns about his problem with Favre but conceded that Brett was possibly the toughest player in the entire NFL; and Browning Nagle, coveted by Glanville over Favre in the '91 draft and selected by the Jets as a consolation prize, had become the No. 3 quarterback in Atlanta.

The way the scenario played out, a lot of people got to say they told you so: Wolf, Holmgren, Herock, Jones, Bower. Everybody but Jerry Glanville.

One point that can't be argued is that, unlike Atlanta the previous season, the Packers were willing to give Favre every chance to prove himself immediately when he arrived in 1992.

In fact, while everyone remembers the dramatic, last-second touchdown pass that beat Cincinnati in the third game that season, very few recall that Favre was tossed into battle a week earlier — or that a brewing quarterback controversy actually was averted when Majkowski injured his knee and Favre took the reins for good.

The Packers lost their opener to Minnesota under Holmgren, then got bombed 31-3 at Tampa Bay. Majkowski, who had been considered the toast of

Wisconsin — Majik Man — as recently as 1989 when the Pack was 10-6, couldn't produce a point in the first half against the Bucs. Favre played the entire second half and completed 8 of 14 passes for 73 yards with one interception.

And Majik was angry.

"I didn't agree with the switch," he said. "I still wanted to go in there. We were only down by 17. I've been in games where we were down by a lot more than that. We could have made some adjustments for the second half."

Holmgren tried to downplay the hubbub. "Some bad things happened in the first half and they weren't always Don's fault," he said. "The game, the way it was going, I thought: What the heck? I wanted to play Brett sometime this season. Early in the season, perhaps."

Needless to say, a competitor like Favre — especially since he'd languished an entire year on the bench in Atlanta — loved the shot at some game action and conceded right off that he wanted more.

"I really want to play now," he said. "It's easier (sitting out) when you haven't gotten in the game yet. You're like, 'Well, my time will come.' But now I've gotten a chance to play. I want to get back in. It's tough. I'm chomping at the bit."

There have been so many mysterious turning points in Brett Favre's career, you can get dizzy playing, "What if?"

But here are some questions to ponder: When would Favre eventually have gotten a fair chance to run the Green Bay offense if Majkowski hadn't wrecked his knee the third week against Cincinnati? Did Holmgren's decision to bench

Majik and give Brett some time under fire at Tampa fuel the kid's confidence and help contribute to a sensational comeback win over the Bengals?

We'll never know.

What's right there on tape and in the Packer record books, though, is that fascinating rally against Cincinnati, the jump-start to what, so far, has been a career on a relentless rise.

Favre threw two fourth-quarter touchdowns in that stirring victory, wrapping up a day on which he completed 22 of 39 passes for 289 yards after Majkowski went down in the first quarter.

Everyone who watched the Packers' final drive, and even those who participated in it, thought Favre exuded nothing but confidence, that pulling things out was simply in the cards. Even when Cincinnati's Jim Breech knocked home a 41-yard field goal with 1:07 left to put the Bengals up 23-17, nobody wavered.

"We had it in our minds even before that kick that it didn't matter," Packers center James Campen said. "Who cared if he made it? We were going to score a touchdown and win."

OK, now the amazing part of that whole story is that Favre — the man who wouldn't lose in the fourth quarter — was really a wreck when he entered the game.

"I was shaky and nervous, knowing what was on the line," he said. "I was the guy. Everybody was counting on me. Honestly, I felt like I was going to have diarrhea. Thank God I held it 'til after the game."

Of course, Favre might have calmed down his teammates by telling them he knew just how to handle feeling rotten and taking over at quarterback. Bad stomachs and surprise victories can get along.

Way back in 1987, when he was a freshman at Southern Mississippi, third-stringer Favre came off the bench to lead his team to a victory over Tulane. He was the starter from then on. But it turns out Brett was feeling pretty darn queasy that afternoon he made his big college breakthrough.

It seems Favre and his roommate were playing a drinking game called "Quarters" the night before in their room. The idea is to bounce a quarter into a glass of beer, but since no quarters were available, they were using a metal washer they'd pried off the sink.

During the night, Favre and his pal polished off an entire case of beer ("Schaefer Light. Six bucks a case," he said...). So imagine how the 17-year-old quarterback felt when he got the call to warm up. Excited, but by his admission, ready to throw up.

"It's like 95 degrees in Hattiesburg," Favre said, "and both our quarterbacks are playing awful, so coach says to me, 'Get in there.' Oh, my stomach. But I go in and throw two touchdown passes, we come from behind and beat them. My roommate says, 'Damn, I know you were hurting.'

"But somehow, I played. Back then it probably relaxed me. I was so nervous all the time. (During the game) I was more worried about the hangover."

By now, of course, Packer fans all know that Favre is ready to play under any circumstances. He's proven he can stay up late and win on Sundays, that he can throw five touchdown passes on an ankle that won't move, that he'll spit up blood and walk back into the huddle.

Brett's next challenge is to show he can perform the same magic without any serious pain medication. Or a six-pack to make the aches go away.

"That's just fine," he said. "You know, in the last couple of years, I've gotten older and the only thing still going strong late at night has been my reputation. I've been home in bed. I always liked the image of a guy like Bobby Layne or Billy Kilmer, who could party 'til morning and then play great, but I've had my share of that now. I'd just as soon go to sleep and get up to play football feeling great.

"It was scary enough going out to play my first big pro game and worrying about diarrhea. After that, what's pressure?"

CHAPTER EIGHT: THE ODD COUPLE

If Mike Holmgren ever wondered what the future might hold with Brett Favre quarterbacking his Green Bay Packers, he probably got a hint right off the bat.

The first time Holmgren summoned the strong-armed country boy to step in for starter Don Majkowski — against Tampa Bay the second week of the 1992 season — Favre immediately cut loose a very memorable pass which resulted in his first NFL completion.

Of course, the ball was batted into the air at the line of scrimmage and Favre had to fight off a crowd to catch it himself. He was promptly buried by Bucs tackle Ray Seals for a 7-yard loss.

Favre to Favre.

No doubt Holmgren rolled his eyes and, if he were a man given to premonitions, perhaps he knew straight-away what was coming down the road. Wild things were *always* going to happen with this new gunner in town.

Favre might be the answer to the Packers' dreams of rebuilding toward another championship era, but this particular quarterback — the man who could make dreams come true — never would be a robot simply running the "West Coast" offense from the pages of his playbook.

Brett always was going to be a different kind of guy, and Holmgren knew it from the beginning.

This is not to say, however, that Holmgren wasn't wholeheartedly in favor of the controversial 1992 trade that fetched Favre from the bench in Atlanta in exchange for a first-round draft pick. Technically, such a transaction belongs on the ledger of the general manager — in this case, Ron Wolf — but no GM in his right mind would give a No. 1 choice for a quarterback who couldn't co-exist with the team's long-term choice as head coach.

Atlanta had made that exact mistake taking Favre in the first place, when general manager Ken Herock overruled coach Jerry Glanville (who preferred Louisville's Browing Nagle) and selected Favre. Glanville responded with a fit of pique and stuck Favre directly in his personal doghouse, which didn't help either the Falcons or their disenchanted No. 3 quarterback.

"It's pretty easy to sit here now and say I really liked the deal when we found out we had a chance to get Brett," Holmgren said. "A few years later, we all look like geniuses because he's turned into the league's MVP and taken us to the championship level.

"But the truth is that the whole thing was pretty risky, both for Ron and me, when we made the trade for Brett.

Mike Holmgren is every bit as strong willed as Favre or any of the
other Packers — and besides, he's the man in charge.

Ron had just been given the full responsibilities for running the most historic football operation in America a few months before, and right away he hired me — a guy with no head-coaching experience in the NFL. Then we turned around, even though we had (Don) Majkowski still on the team with all the things he'd accomplished, and shipped out a No. 1 draft choice for a third-stringer in Atlanta. Reaction in Green Bay was, well...I don't remember them staging a ticker-tape parade when the trade was announced.

"I can't speak for Ron, but I could have been back teaching high school faster than I ever planned if that deal had gone completely wrong. Still, I have tremendous respect for Ron's judgment — that's one of the things that made the Green Bay job so enticing to me — and he was absolutely sold on Brett. Ron never wavered on that.

"And frankly, I agreed with him. The offense we were going to run required somebody who was tough, bright, with a good arm and the type of leadership qualities that can move you up from the middle of the pack to the level we wanted to reach. That was the thing: Brett was unproven as a professional, but everything Ron and I had seen of him indicated that he had a tremendous upside.

"In this business, if you settle for playing it safe, you'll never be better than average and pretty soon, you're gone. Our goal wasn't to be mediocre, it was to win a Super Bowl, and to do that in our offense, we needed a big-time quarterback. We didn't mind getting one we had to teach — that's probably the best situation, anyway, finding somebody with the right tools and molding the guy yourself."

Over the course of their relationship, Holmgren may have had to adjust his meaning of the word "mold," but there's no question he and Favre have provided exactly what the other needed.

Which is not to say there weren't some times when Holmgren drove home muttering to himself. A lot of times, actually.

"Looking back, I probably drove Mike crazy more than once," Favre said with a laugh. "I've always been the kind of guy who questions authority. I did it with my dad when he was coaching me in high school. I'm sure Mike can tell you a lot of stories about him telling me something and having it go in one ear and right out the other."

Besides whatever fuss might be caused by Favre's do-it-my-way nature, he and Holmgren were bound to clash over the actual execution of the Packer offense. They did and, occasionally, they still do.

Favre absolutely loves the role of make-it-happen improviser. He'd just as soon draw plays in the dirt, scramble around forever while the crowd goes wild and then uncork some bomb that nobody expects. Or just reverse field and go dashing into a swarm of linebackers himself.

Needless to say, that doesn't exactly fit the job description in the offense Holmgren helped implement during all those successful years with the 49ers. The attack Holmgren brought to Green Bay involved scripted scenarios, a carefully drawn-up series of moves and counter-moves designed to free receivers and move the chains — if

photo by Vernon Biever

Quarterbacks coach Stever Mariucci helped Brett develop and maintain
his confidence during some rough spots early on, and the two men
became close friends. Mariucci left the staff after the 1995 season
to become head coach at the University of California.

the quarterback simply followed instructions and made decisions in the order he'd been taught.

Mike Holmgren, in other words, wasn't looking for sandlot football. Which was Favre's favorite kind.

So how did this odd couple survive and flourish?

"The important thing for me is to stay one step ahead of him," Favre said, tongue only partially in cheek. "Here's Mike from San Francisco and I'm from the bayou. He's cultured and I'm country. He went to USC and I went to USM. He probably eats calamari and I eat crawfish.

"So coming from a background like that, you know he thinks he's smarter than I am. But that's OK, because I always know what he's going to do before he does it. He's a pretty sharp guy, but with me, he's chasing a fast rabbit and I'll always be just a little ahead."

Favre broke down and laughed aloud at his description of the relationship. He would have howled listening to Holmgren's version, which is pretty much the opposite.

"I know how clever Brett thinks he is," Holmgren said. "And truthfully, he really *is* a very sharp guy. You can't survive, let alone be a star, playing quarterback in the NFL if you aren't pretty bright. But sometimes, dealing with him reminds me of the kids I taught in high school. The smart ones will always challenge you, always want to change something around to have it their way, and the key for the teacher is to stay in control without taking away any of the student's talent or creativity.

"That's the situation we have here. But trust me when I tell you I'm still the coach, and *I am* in control."

Holmgren certainly has had plenty of chances to prove it. He's had to call Favre in for lectures so many times, both men have lost count.

"A couple of times, he's gotten me to the point where I wanted to go right through the roof," Holmgren said. "After the 1993 season, when he threw those 24 interceptions but we made the playoffs anyway, Brett told some reporter that he wasn't going to change his style, that the offense was good but he was the kind of playmaker, some riverboat gambler who had to take crazy chances sometimes and that's just how it was. The gist of his remarks was that we were a better team because he went off winging it on his own a lot of the time instead of sticking with what the coaching staff wanted to do.

"Oh, I was hot. I sat him down and I was really mad. I told him, 'Look, you think that running around the field and throwing stupid interceptions is the way to go. Well, where it got us was a 9-7 record. Is that what you want, to be 9-7? Because I guarantee you that if you don't learn more and more about this offense, and run it the way you're supposed to, I don't care how many spectacular plays you make every once in awhile, you'll always be a 9-7 quarterback.'

"It's fair to say that was a heated exchange. But I was right and I think, deep down, he *knew* I was right. Here's a guy with all that talent, and if he applies himself properly and executes things in the right framework, maybe we're going to get to the Super Bowl. But playing like a kid on the street? No way."

What came from that trip to the principal's office was something of a compromise: Favre definitely has thrown himself into learning every nuance of Holmgren's deadly offense and now he's running it with the savvy of a young Joe Montana or Steve Young.

On the other hand, Holmgren has learned to give a little, too. He allows Favre more flexibility in the offense than he'd give almost any other quarterback. The result is that, once in awhile, Holmgren suffers near heart failure when plays fall apart and Favre runs everywhere but to the popcorn stand. But Holmgren also has come to trust that, in those moments of individual artistry, Favre also will deliver him some wonderful results.

By 1995, Holmgren had reached the point where — even if it wasn't textbook stuff — he could almost *enjoy* one of Favre's run-right, spin-left, throw-underhanded completions. After Brett improbably eluded two rushers on one play, managed a 360-degree turn and somehow found a receiver open for the touchdown, Holmgren walked up to him on the sideline and said, "You know, I think that's the greatest play I've ever seen."

Favre was thrilled.

"Imagine, Mike telling me that," Favre said. "Two or three years ago, that kind of play would have put him in the hospital. But now maybe he trusts me more. When he said it was the best play he'd ever seen, that got me more pumped up than even scoring the touchdown."

Student pleases teacher.

Still, these two confident men — each proud and certain

of their own skills — are bound to differ on subject after subject. And Favre, who is one of the most outspoken athletes on earth, isn't going to just sit in his locker stall and be quiet about it.

For instance, when all-pro wide receiver Sterling Sharpe was forced to retire because of a neck injury following the 1994 season and the Packers promptly responded with an 11-5 regular-season record in '95, Favre announced to one and all that the team didn't miss Sharpe. In fact, the quarterback said, Sharpe's departure speeded up his own development because it helped him look over the entire field instead of standing in the pocket and searching for his superstar.

Holmgren claims that's balderdash.

"Brett was going to take the next step anyway," Holmgren said, "simply because he had another year in the league and another year learning what essentially is a very complicated offense. Brett was getting better and better because it was coming easier to him, finding the second option and the third option.

"Frankly, I would have preferred that Sterling Sharpe had still been around as one of those options. Are you kidding? Sterling was a great player. Imagine Brett with all he's learned, the way he's grasping things now, *and* having a Sterling Sharpe as part of the package.

"Brett and the media can paint this any way they like, but I can tell you absolutely that losing Sterling didn't speed up Brett's emergence as the MVP. He did it himself, through experience to go with his God-given talent."

And so on.

Even when things have been going good, Holmgren has found himself having to smack Favre's wrist with a ruler — figuratively speaking.

During the Pack's 1995 run to the NFC Central Division championship, Favre was on his way to 38 touchdown passes and almost unanimous acclaim as the most exciting young quarterback in football. And *still* Holmgren had to scold him when Brett was quoted near the end of the year saying he "deserved" to be the league's MVP.

"Yeah, we had to have another one of our little talks about that," Holmgren recalled with a sigh. "I tried to explain to him that it was a lot better to put up the numbers and win football games, then let other people tell you how good you are. He didn't need to campaign for himself."

Favre's response? "He told me he was just giving an honest answer to a question," Holmgren said, grinning. "And I had to concede it was honest. Not the way I'd handle it exactly, but honest."

An outsider might look at the Packer hierarchy and wonder how Holmgren and Favre managed to survive together, especially those first two or three years. Other coach-quarterback beefs have broken teams apart — remember the sideline explosion between Raiders quarterback Jeff Hostetler and soon-to-be-fired coach Art Shell?

A couple of things allowed the Green Bay relationship to become smoother than the two personalities made it appear.

First off, both Holmgren and Favre — however different their backgrounds — are genuinely likable characters. Neither holds a grudge nor is the least bit mean-spirited. So when heads knocked over this pass or that audible or whatever, the issue could be fussed over and then forgotten.

In fact, coach and quarterback actually have something in common that is far stronger than their divergent opinions about whether and when Brett ought to flee the pocket and try to create something for the highlight film: Each man aches to win.

"One thing that helped a lot in working with Brett," Holmgren said, "is that I coached Steve Young. Not once, but twice. I had him at BYU (when Holmgren was quarterback coach under LaVell Edwards from 1982-85) and we won the national championship in '84 with Steve there. Then obviously, I worked with Steve during my time in San Francisco.

"He and Brett are so much alike in a lot of ways. Forget about the fact that Steve is a Mormon and all that — the guy is a fierce battler. And he's every bit as hard-headed as Brett. Thinks he knows more about it than you do. He's a tough case, which is the mark of a lot of great ones. They want to win so badly, they set incredible expectations for themselves and they can be hard on everybody.

"Steve was a super talent, obviously, but with the 49ers, especially, you had to prove to him that the system would work. In his case, he had to learn that he didn't have to take off and run with the ball — no matter how great a runner he is — every time the first receiver was covered.

Favre has his sights set on greatness, so it doesn't hurt to rub elbows with
Hall of Famers like former Bears quarterback Sid Luckman.

"You notice that when Steve became a truly outstanding quarterback and eventually won a Super Bowl, he'd come to trust the system first and then use his own special skills only when everything else broke down.

"That's the lesson I wanted Brett to understand, that sure, he could do some amazing things inventing plays on the fly. He could scramble and make unbelievable throws. But we wanted him to stick with the system, learn it as completely as he could and take all the easy stuff first. And *then* look for Plan B. Even throw the ball away if he had to, and Brett would rather go to the dentist than just give up on a play and throw the ball out of bounds.

"But he's getting there, he really is. I think he proved it last year. People still think of Brett as this wild guy taking big risks, but look at his touchdowns-to-interceptions ratio the past two years (71 to 17). You don't put up numbers like that making many stupid plays."

Another thing that made the Holmgren-Favre marriage easier those first four years was the presence of quarterback coach Steve Mariucci. Brett not only trusted Mariucci and learned from him, but the Packer staff more or less decided to let Holmgren and Mariucci play good cop-bad cop with their young quarterback.

"He (Mariucci) could always reach out to me," Favre said. "He told me from the very first year, when I was really unsure of myself sometimes in the offense, that eventually I was going to be the most valuable player in the NFL. He said that over and over. He really believed in me and never wavered, so if Mike was upset or I'd thrown a bad ball that was picked off and really hurt us, Steve was there to explain it, to work with me on it or learn from it. Sometimes it was as simple as just being my friend.

"Steve was the perfect coach for me at that time, and not just because we could kid each other and we got along so well, either. He really knew how to teach me, to explain things just the right way without taking away any of my confidence."

Mariucci left the Packers after the '95 season to take the head coaching job at the University of California, causing some consternation about how Favre — coming off the rehab ordeal — would deal with the changing landscape.

"Maybe (Mariucci) decided I was grown up enough that he could leave me on my own without a babysitter," Favre joked. "No, seriously, Steve deserved that job and I'll be fine without him. I've been in the league long enough now to understand what's going on.

"But I'm sure glad he was around when he was. There were times when Mike would get on me and I'd get mad and throw down my helmet and say, 'What a jerk.' Then a few minutes later, Mike would say something nice and I'd go, 'Aw, he's not a bad guy.' Back and forth. You know, I'm only 26 now. I was just a kid then and I didn't realize some of what was happening. So it was good to have Steve around as my pal."

Holmgren can laugh now about some of the trying times he endured with his gifted young quarterback. "It was like raising one of your own kids," he said. "You love 'em, and then they do something that makes you crazy. So you try to correct it. But you still love 'em."

The relationship clearly has entered a new phase as Holmgren and Favre set their sights on football's ultimate prize.

"To give you an example," Holmgren said, "by last year (1995), I really wasn't working with Brett so much on the offense anymore. I didn't talk to him as much about reads and defenses and all of that as I did about maturity, about growing into the role of superstar.

"Take the way he dresses. Brett's the worst dresser I've ever seen, but back home that's how he's comfortable. Great. But here we are, a professional football team on a road trip or something, and Brett would look like he just crawled out of a swamp in Mississippi.

"Finally, I told him, 'Listen, you aren't just a kid from the country anymore. You're one of the biggest stars in the NFL. You don't just represent yourself now, you represent me, the Packers, the league. When we go into a hotel in New York or someplace, there are hundreds of people there, and they're all wondering which one is Brett Favre. And there you are, with cut-offs, sandals and a T-shirt with a hole in it.'

"So the next time we took a road trip, we're getting ready to take off and I'm doing my head coach thing, you know, walking back through the plane to joke a little here and there, talk to the fellas. And I see Brett, and he's wearing a coat and tie. I told him, 'Hey, you really look nice.'

"But the funny thing was that he reminded me of that kid you knew in grade school, little Freddy who was always a mess and then they made him dress up one day a year for the school picture. Brushed his hair and the whole bit. That's how Brett looked, liked Freddy in the class picture, fiddling with his collar and everything like, 'Man, I can't *wait* to get out of this stuff.' "

Much more important than cleaning up his star's sartorial act, however, was the role Holmgren played when the news broke about Favre's painkiller addiction. It was a dicey time for everyone involved — media descended on the Packers like so many swarms of locust — and Holmgren stepped into the breech.

Holmgren is imposing enough (6-5, 240 pounds) on a happy day, but when Favre's health and his privacy were at stake, the coach became an unscalable wall between the prying world and his quarterback.

Not only did Holmgren interrupt his only vacation of the year to visit Favre during Brett's six-week treatment at the Menninger Clinic — impressing Favre mightily — the coach also announced point-blank that Brett would have no contact with the press until the team could orchestrate a press conference at which he, Holmgren, would preside.

During that session, Holmgren ran the show like a protective father, turning aside questions he deemed too personal or intrusive into Favre's right of privacy under NFL guidelines. Several times, Holmgren placed a cautioning hand on Favre's shoulder to halt a line of questioning before it could even get going.

"I was worried that I might come off as being too heavy-handed with the media," Holmgren said afterward, "but the alternative was to let everybody loose with a young man who just got out of treatment, whose health was at stake and whose nature is to answer whatever you ask him. If the media wanted to criticize me, fine, but I wasn't going to let that happen to Brett."

It was time, in other words, for Favre to feel the big man's strength fully behind him.

"It's funny to go back a few years and think of the little battles and misunderstandings we've had," Favre said. "It's easy to laugh about it now, because I'm older and I can see where Mike's coming from. He's been on my side all along. I'd say we have a very solid relationship."

And then a smile.

"But that doesn't mean I won't cause Mike to lose a few more hairs on the sideline," Favre joked. "The ones he's got left."

CHAPTER NINE:
SUPERMAN

So after four years under center in the National Football League, Brett Favre is a star.

But really, how do you describe this unique quarterback?

Oh, the numbers are all there, sure enough: He's thrown 71 touchdowns against just 17 interceptions in the two seasons prior to 1996 — the second-best two-year ratio in that category in league history.

Favre already owns the league's fourth-best career passer rating (86.8) and passing efficiency percentage (62.4), and his 14,825 total yards has catapulted him to third place on the all-time Packer passing list behind Bart Starr, who played 16 seasons, and Lynn Dickey, who played nine. If he stays reasonably healthy and doesn't suddenly decide to retire to the shores of Rotten Bayou, Favre almost surely will own every passing record in the franchise's glorious 78-year history.

"It's really silly to talk about things like this after just a few seasons, especially since we haven't even won a Super

Bowl yet," Favre said, "but I admit one of my goals is to be in the Hall of Fame.

"Why shouldn't I aim for that? When you go back and look where I came from, the odds were probably longer that I'd even make it into the NFL when I was in high school than the odds against the Hall of Fame are now. Besides, I always want to shoot for the top and, right after winning championships, the Hall of Fame would be the highest achievement."

Yes, the numbers, statistics and certainly the potential for status as a pro football legend are all right there for anyone to see. So is Favre's outright ambition to be the best.

But what about his style?

How do those who know the NFL best assess this remarkable talent in terms of *how* he's going about this business of becoming a megastar? Who would you compare him to?

Dickey, for one, admitted he was stumped trying to put Favre into a particular category.

"I grew up watching a lot of great quarterbacks in the 1950s and 60s," he said. "I played myself in the '70s and '80s, and obviously I've been observing all the good ones recently. But I've seen Brett an awful lot and believe me, it's hard to think of anyone he really resembles. There are parts of his game that make you think of one guy and other parts that suggest somebody else, but then Brett does something that just says, 'Hey, I'm one of a kind.'

"It's so strange because quarterbacks usually do fit some kind of mold. Either they're straight drop-back guys, or

When he isn't throwing touchdown passes,
Favre isn't above looking cool on the sidelines.

scramblers. They have particular throwing motions that remind you of someone else. They're noticeably tall or short, they have great touch or powerhouse arms or whatever it is that puts them in a particular category.

"But I see Brett and sometimes I just shake my head. For instance, just take his throwing motion. There's something unusual there. Very unusual. I've watched and tried to pull it apart, piece by piece, over the years. And sometimes I just can't believe what I'm seeing.

"OK, he's got the great arm strength. Everybody knows that. It's the type of thing that comes from throwing rocks and eggs and whatever else you do when you're a kid. I know because I did it myself. You're always aiming at some can or something and saying, 'Can I hit this from here? Or maybe from way back here?'

"The crazy part, though, is that through the years, the most successful quarterbacks — not counting the Billy Kilmers and those pure-guts guys — have been technically sound. I mean, there's a right way to deliver the football accurately with something on it. Technique matters, it matters a lot.

"But with Brett, sometimes you see him get his ass and legs positioned properly, and he really unloads the balls with big-time zip. But then other times, you see him moving one way with his body all twisted around and he throws the ball — I mean, hard — in completely the other direction. That's just all arm. And you think, *nobody* can have an arm so strong that the rest of his technique doesn't matter at all.

"But I can show you throws to prove that Brett does things that no quarterback I've ever seen would even try."

Dickey threw for 21,369 yards in a Green Bay uniform, including a club-record 4,458 in 1983, so he certainly qualifies as an expert discussing the position. Yet Dickey concedes he couldn't imagine completing some of the throws Favre executes with regularity.

"Let me give you an example," Dickey said. "Say your primary receiver is on the left. You turn your body in that direction. Now you see that guy is covered, so you want to go back to the right. What I was taught, from the time I was a little kid, was that you pivot to get yourself realigned, step and throw back to the right.

"When you see Brett in that situation, sometimes he won't even move his feet when he decides to throw in a different direction. He doesn't really move and step into the pass, he just somehow rotates his upper body and fires. He can do that and put the ball on a line for 40 or 50 yards. You shouldn't be able to do that."

Dickey tries and tries, but he can't quite make a comparison between Favre and any other quarterback.

"One guy who comes to mind is Terry Bradshaw," Dickey said. "There was another big, strong guy with the cannon arm. Terry threw the ball off his back foot once in awhile when he was first in the NFL, but basically, whether he was standing in the pocket or rolling out, he still had the step-up-and-fire delivery. I don't know that even Bradshaw had the arm strength to do what Brett does.

"It's like you look at Brett and see some of Dan Marino's quick release, some of (Joe) Montana's ability to move in the pocket by just somehow *feeling* the rush, and definitely some of that Steve Young toughness and knack for escaping, then either throwing the ball or just tearing upfield with it.

"Still, he's also different from each of those in some ways, too. He isn't supposed to be fast, but Brett always seems to be able to outrun the guys he needs to for a first down or the end zone. Obviously, Brett can throw the ball about as far as anybody, but now he's also learned to spot an open guy at the last second and really put a soft touch on the ball. And all with a motion that, honestly, I've never seen before."

Favre himself doesn't claim to understand his throwing technique. While he spends hours studying opponents and learning the nuances of the famous "West Coast" offense, Brett simply seems just to trust his arm to get the ball wherever it's supposed to go.

Even when you ask him to stand still and demonstrate how he throws the ball, Favre seems as interested — or puzzled — as any questioner.

"When I look at films of other quarterbacks, it does seem like the guys who throw hard really take a big wind-up," Brett said, "and I don't do that. To me, it seems like a throw like a catcher in baseball. I see myself on film and the ball never gets back much past my ear. Like I just pull it back a little ways and throw. To tell the truth, I don't know how I can throw it so hard. I'm just glad I can."

When the subject of other quarterbacks comes up, Favre's link to the 49ers' Young is inescapable, and not just because he has been tutored by Mike Holmgren. Besides being hard-headed guys who really wanted to stray from

One of the most amazing things about Favre is that despite growing
up in balmy Mississippi, he's been at his best for the Packers
when temperatures have been chilly.

planned offensive patterns — more earlier in their careers than later — Favre and Young are rough-and-tumble types who could have played in the leather-helmet era.

"I think we both have a side to us that would run into a brick wall if we could get a first down or help our team," Young said. "In fact, we've both probably tried that, with some sort of success."

When the Packers were getting ready to face Young and Co. in the 1995 playoffs, 49ers linebacker Gary Plummer observed: "The analysis I've made all week is that Favre reminds me of Steve Young now. Whereas back then (Favre's first couple of seasons), he looked like Steve Young in the USFL, scrambling to run the ball. Now he's moving around the pocket to be able to throw the ball.

"I don't know if the Packers have the same play Steve had in the USFL, where they just snap it over his head and let him run back there, pick it up and see what happens."

The Packers don't, but however more controlled he's become the past year or two, Favre no doubt would love it.

When Favre is asked about comparisons to other quarterbacks, on the other hand, he doesn't respond in terms of style or throwing motion. Brett wants to be mentioned in the same breath with consistent winners — like Young. Brett considers championships and consistency the true measures of a quarterback's success.

"When you think of Bradshaw or (Roger) Staubach, you think of Super Bowls, not stats," Favre said. "I can't tell you Bradshaw's stats, but I can tell you he's 4-0 in the Super Bowl. What people will care about is how many wins I have.

Things like consecutive starts (he opened 1996 with a league-best 68 in a row) mean something to me. I want people to look back and say, 'He was a winner and he was fun as hell to watch.' "

Brett returned to that same theme when asked about his definition of leadership.

"Winner. Durability," he said. "You have to make plays you're not supposed to make. A lot of people say a leader is a guy that gets his team fired up. I totally disagree. I'm not one of those vocal guys before a game, as much as I like to talk. I think it's the guy, like (John) Elway, who can kind of do the impossible and is there time and time again."

Ironically, though, Favre's favorite quarterbacks have something else in common besides being winners. They're entertainers — a description he *never* wants to lose — and a lot of them are throwbacks to the days when NFL quarterbacks were beer-swilling characters who played hard off the field and on it.

Favre understands full well that his long-standing reputation as a party animal who could still deliver at game time — greatly exaggerated the past year or two, he claims — must now be altered completely in the wake of his bout with painkiller addiction. But he still loves all those stories about guys like Bobby Layne, Sonny Jurgensen, Kilmer and others who just did it their own way and still walked away winners.

"I'm not going to lie and say that wasn't the way I pictured myself when I was younger," he said. "In college, I was famous for it. But I look back now and think, 'Gawd,

Favre loves the image of a tough-guy quarterback who can't stand to lose.

you drank six beers the night before a game.' I wanted people to remember me as a great quarterback. But what you always got was, 'Did you hear about him the other night?' "

Even prior to the 1995 season, when the painkiller business finally got out of hand, Favre still had his let's-party moments, and naturally, they fed the reputation he'd developed as a wild and crazy guy who could still shred defenses on Sundays.

During the spring of '95, Brett played in a one-day golf shootout with other NFL quarterbacks, an event held in conjunction with a PGA Senior Tour stop in New Jersey. Favre was paired with Stan Humphries, who took his golf pretty seriously, but nonetheless Brett and a few friends stayed up most of the previous night enjoying the nightlife of New York City.

"I showed up, and I'm hurting," Favre said. "I'm trying to look like I'm with it, but it's cold and windy and raining. Stan's out there real serious — 'C'mon, let's sink this putt...' — and I'm like, 'I need a Coke.' We wound up winning $25,000 apiece."

That story would be music to the ears of somebody like Kilmer, for whom Favre admitted having great admiration. Brett was too young to see Kilmer play in person, but he watched a TV show one night that featured the former 49er and Redskins star — and Brett was in awe.

"His shirttail is hanging out," Favre said of Kilmer. "He's got a little pot belly. If he didn't have a uniform on, you'd think he was some janitor or truck driver. His nose was smashed up. There was tape all over it. He had blood all down his jersey, his arms, his sweatbands. His eyes were kind of swollen around his nose.

"Then he scrambles around for a 20-yard play, dives into the end zone. I got chill bumps. How'd he do it? He can't outrun anybody. He's slower than I am, which is bad. But he found a way to do it. That's what separates the great ones from the average ones."

Favre insists there is more to the comparisons with a guy like Kilmer or Layne than the fact that he used to drink a few beers.

"There are some quarterbacks that can outrun me, probably out-throw me, ones that are more accurate," he said. "But why aren't you hearing about them? What separates me from some other guy who's the same size as me, same speed, same arm and everything? It's the fire inside, the emotion. I love to play the game.

"Picking up the paychecks is fun, but it's more fun for me to go out and play the game. I hate during the week, practicing and waiting for Sunday to come. Then when Sunday comes, I have to control myself."

There is plenty of evidence, right there on Packer game tapes, to prove Favre's contention. Sure, you can see plenty of laser throws, long bombs and out-pattern zingers.

But Brett is prouder, for instance, of the game-winning touchdown he scored in the final seconds against Atlanta in 1994, a late-season matchup that lifted the Packers into the playoffs. Sure, he made some great throws to fuel the winning drive, but what really excites Brett is recalling the broken play and lumbering run he made to score the clinching TD.

"No way I'm faster than the two guys who were chasing me," Brett said, "but I had to get in the end zone and I did it. That's the kind of football I want to be remembered for."

That, or perhaps the 24-19 triumph over Pittsburgh in the final regular-season game of 1995. The Packers needed a win to wrap up their first NFC Central Division title since 1972, and to get it, Favre survived two tremendous hits. The first knocked him out of the game — backup Jim McMahon played briefly — and the next, down near the goal line with the game on the line, sent Favre to the sidelines with blood running out of his mouth.

That collision prompted one of the more fascinating sideline exchanges in football history.

"The trainer came up to me and told me, 'Brett's spitting up blood,'" coach Mike Holmgren said. "I asked him, 'How much?'

"I mean, people have made a big deal of my saying that — John Madden talked about it on TV — but hey, football is a rough game and I've seen a lot of blood. I really wanted to know: Is this something serious, where I've got to get McMahon in there, or is it just a little blood and if we take a time-out to let him catch his breath, Brett can go back in. It wasn't like I was sending this mortally wounded guy out to get killed.

"They told me it wasn't too bad. Brett said he was ready to go, and he went back in and threw the winning touchdown pass. The only guy who got upset was McMahon, because he knew the play we had called would work and he wanted the touchdown."

Favre: "Jimmy Mac still gets on me about that. He told me I was hogging all the glory. I loved it. But so did he. Mac would have done the same thing because he's that kind of player, too."

There are a couple of other aspects to Favre's particular brand of leadership that mean a lot to him, as well.

The first is that he believes a great quarterback absolutely *must* have the confidence of his teammates, and that's something Brett has enjoyed since high school. At every level of play, guys have rallied around him.

"When Brett jumps in the huddle, maybe he's joking or telling a funny story, or maybe he's pointing out some funny guy in the stands," Packer center Frank Winters said, "but however he does it, he makes every single guy there feel like there's no way we can't go right down the field. It doesn't matter if we've got a whole quarter or 15 seconds. You feel with Brett in there, you're going to get it done.

"Sometime you can look at another team that has the ball at the end, and our defense is trying to shut them down, and you can just tell that they don't have the confidence to score. You can see it in their eyes and their body language. With Brett, we're just the opposite. We *always* think we're going to win, no matter what the situation is."

Green Bay running back Edgar Bennett explained a

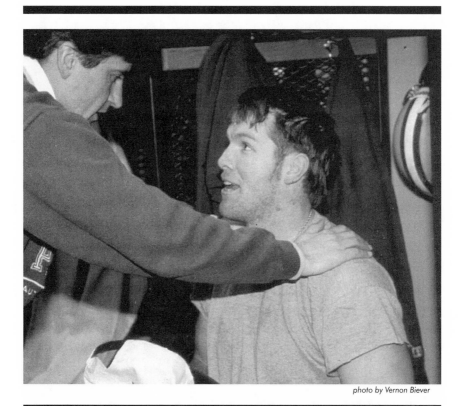

photo by Vernon Biever

Brett's coaches and teammates all insist he projects
confidence into everyone around him.

unique phenomenon: how Favre can excite and relax his team simultaneously.

"When Brett steps into the huddle, he fires everyone up," Bennett said. "But at the same time, he calms you down. He'll say, 'Just give me time and I'll get it done.' And he will. If we block for him and give him time, he'll shred any defense."

Favre's old buddy from Southern Mississippi, 300-pound lineman Chris Ryals, noticed the same thing. "Brett just steps up and takes over," Ryals said, "and everybody knew we were going to score. The way that works, with somebody like Brett, everybody is always going to put his body on the line to block a little harder, give a little more. He's one of us, and we know he'll do anything to win, too, so you have that added desire to do whatever it takes. Brett's the kind of quarterback who is just one of the boys, but you also know he's got that special something, and if you just do your job, he'll win the game for you."

One of the boys.

Now there's the other part of the leadership equation that comes so naturally to Favre.

"The first time I met him," Winters said, "I'd just come to the Packers from Kansas City on Plan B, so I didn't know many of the guys. It turned out that was right about the time the Packers traded for Brett. Everybody knew about the trade, and here was this quarterback of the future coming in, and guys are all talking about him.

"I just happened to be sitting down to eat when this guy comes over and sits down at the table. He looked pretty big, and he had a lumberjack shirt or something like that on, and I thought he was a linebacker. I said, 'Hey, I'm Frank Winters,' and he goes, 'Hi, I'm Brett Favre.'

"This was our new quarterback and I wouldn't have picked him out of a crowd at all. He didn't even look like a quarterback, or act like somebody important. From the first day, he was just one of the guys and we got to be friends right away. He and I and Mark (Chmura) all sort of arrived around the same time and started hanging out together. I thought it was kind of funny because you don't see too many linemen and quarterbacks going out together very often, but that's Brett. If he couldn't throw the ball the way he does, he *would* be a linebacker or strong safety or something. He was just a football player, you know?"

Plenty of stories already have been documented about some of the antics Favre, Winters and Chmura have dreamed up — they are Green Bay's unquestioned prank leaders — but one of the best yarns came about when the Packers had an off week during the 1994 season.

"Chewy (Chmura) had an invitation to go down to Phoenix, where his agent is, to play golf and fool around a little," Favre said. "So I went down there with him. I got it in my head that we should get matching tattoos. I don't even know why I was thinking about it. I just was.

"Well, Chewy didn't want to have anything to do with it. He's saying, 'No way,' but we get down there and I kept going on about the tattoos, and after a few beers, he finally agreed to do it. So we go to this tattoo place and start looking at designs. We didn't see any we liked right away, and finally we asked this guy if he could do a Superman logo.

"The guy said he didn't have the design there, but he could get something to draw it from, and when he showed it to us, we said, 'Yeah, that's us.' So we each got these Superman tattoos on our arms, kind of as a joke.

"The funniest part is that, even though it was my idea in the first place, I felt sort of weird with the thing once we got back to Green Bay. I kind of kept my arm covered whenever I could. But Chewy really got into it. He's got these big guns, and now he wants to show 'em off and flash that tattoo on TV and everything.

"You watch. He's always got short sleeves and whenever he catches a pass, he muscles up and flexes and all that stuff to show off the Superman tattoo. I get on him about it all the time and he denies it, but he loves that thing. He thinks he really is Superman now."

Funny, but that's how a lot of opponents have come to regard Favre.

Ask the New Orleans Saints, who had a game won in '93 until Favre — running for his life to the left — somehow pivoted back, spotted Sterling Sharpe about 50 yards downfield and delivered a miracle strike that set up a game-winning field goal.

Or the Lions, who saw almost that exact same play in the first round of the 1994 playoffs.

Or certainly the Bears, who *had* to figure Favre wouldn't even play after badly spraining his ankle against Minnesota the previous week. Not only did Favre show up, wearing an apparatus almost like a cast that left his foot virtually immobile, he threw five touchdown passes to rally the Packers to a 35-28 victory.

"I couldn't care less how it looks or how I act," Favre said. "I don't want to be like anybody else. I don't want to play like anybody else. I'm not going to do it the way everybody wants me to (another Excedrin for poor Mike Holmgren), including the coach. Bottom line is make plays.

"I do things that '90s quarterbacks don't do. But I really think the game should be fun. People pay a lot of money to watch us play, and I want them to enjoy themselves. I want to play quarterback the way I'd like to see it if I were sitting up there with everybody else, so I'm *always* going to make some crazy plays."

Holmgren has learned to live with it. He knows he'll get far more touchdowns than tragedies, especially now that Favre has become a master of the offense in addition to occasional sandlot showman.

"I just worry that, some of the things Brett does, he's liable to run into a parked Chevy," Holmgren said. "Or a telephone pole."

Nah. That wouldn't happen to Superman.

CHAPTER TEN: HONEYMOON AT THE SUPER BOWL?

Almost all rational human beings eventually must confront the age-old question: Is there life after death?

For professional athletes, the refrain is far more specific and short-term. For instance: Is there life after football?

And now, in the case of Brett Favre, you have the most immediate and pointed question possible: Is there life after Vicodin?

Favre sat smiling and generally upbeat at the press conference marking his return from painkiller treatment at the Menninger Clinic, and assured one and all that he would whip whatever dependency he'd formed for narcotic drugs. Put it in the past. Alcohol, too, if that's what it took.

Moreover, Brett mentioned again and again that he was in the best physical and mental shape of his life, and intended to prove it by leading the Green Bay Packers to the Super Bowl.

Favre conceded that day that he would have his doubters, people who perhaps thought he was a druggie without hope, a party boy who might slug down a few beers and flunk one of the NFL's mandated drug screenings. And he admitted, with a sigh, that whenever he played poorly in 1996 or beyond, the questions would arise: Did he load up? Is he losing it because he can't play *without* the drugs?

The best Favre could do on that particular afternoon — July 17, 1996 — was assure one and all that he felt fine (he certainly looked better than anyone could remember) and that his life, both on the field and off it, was remarkably in order.

To paraphrase the news commentator Paul Harvey, all the rest of us could do is wait for "...the rest of the story."

In the violent world of pro football, you're never guaranteed another play from scrimmage, let alone another week or another year. Quarterbacks make frightening targets as they stare downfield with total disregard for the hordes of 280-pound behemoths bearing down on them at breakneck speed.

Look around the NFL. Check out the superstar quarterbacks, especially the ones who have survived on top the longest: Dan Marino is as gimpy as a codger from surgery; John Elway, likewise; Troy Aikman has suffered so many concussions that doctors fear one more solid jolt could end his career.

"I'm not naive and I'm not bulletproof," Favre has said,

"but I think I'm pretty tough. I love the game, including the physical part. Sure, you take a beating. With all the hits that a quarterback gets, you need a little luck to go out and perform every week, every year. So you hope for some luck. But after that, all you can do is play hard and hope for the best."

Packer coach Mike Holmgren made one thing clear at Favre's post-treatment media session: From now on, if the quarterback needs pain medication, he'll be getting non-addictive (read: less effective) chemicals.

"And then, if I can't play, I just can't play," Favre said.

What you have to conclude from the attitude of Favre, his coaches, the Packers, medical personnel, Brett's teammates and everyone else involved with his profession — which is winning football games — is that everything is in order. Favre enters the 1996 season, and hopefully he'll have many beyond that, as a relatively healthy quarterback ready to start winging the ball down the field.

The other side of the equation, Brett's mental and emotional well-being, is not available for public scrutiny very often. But for a man fighting to recover from the trauma of a drug addiction, what's going on in Favre's heart and soul is probably even more important than sore ribs, an aching knee or whatever.

And fortunately, Brett's peace of mind may be in the best hands of all.

It's impossible, first of all, to understate the importance of his support system, which includes foxhole buddies like Frank Winters and Mark Chmura (along with the rest of

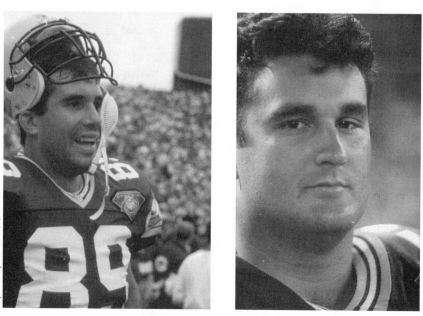

photos by Vernon Biever

Mark Chmura (left) and Frank Winters quickly became Favre's two closest pals on the Packers, and the trio has been involved in plenty of locker-room hijinks. More important, though, they've also stuck together through good times and bad.

the Packers), a bright and sympathetic coach in Holmgren, a warm and loyal family and, finally, the stability of a newly strengthened relationship with his longtime love, the former Deanna Tynes.

Brett and Deanna have been sweethearts since high school, and besides sharing living space, they've been doting parents of a beautiful daughter, Brittany, for going on eight years.

But during Favre's rise to football stardom, Deanna has been forced to play something of a secondary role. During Brett's first three seasons with the Packers, Deanna and Brittany basically stayed home in Mississippi while the man in their lives went about the business of throwing touchdown passes and accepting the adulation of millions.

When Brett came to grief in the grip of Vicodin, however, it was Deanna who stepped up and starting throwing blocks that would do credit to any of the Packer lineman who protect Favre for a living. She was the one who first recognized how scary Brett's Vicodin consumption had become. Deanna not only confronted Brett in no uncertain terms, she took the bold steps of flushing pills down toilets and eventually, contacting Packers doctors with her fears.

In fact, Deanna may have saved her man's life.

"That girl has always been in the background," Frank Winters' wife Aleta said while Brett was still cooped up in the treatment center. "But believe me, she's strong and she's stuck by Brett through some times that had to be difficult — him being a big star with women throwing themselves at his feet everywhere he went. She understood it all and hung in there.

"I really think that one of the things that will come from Brett's admission of this problem and getting help is that his relationship with Deanna will get much, much stronger. I know Brett's kind of resisted getting married, even after all this time they've been together, but I'll bet you see they're married pretty soon.

"Brett knows now what that lady means to him and what an important part she plays in his life and Brittany's life."

At the time, Aleta swore she didn't really know anything for a *fact*. But maybe women just have a way of intuiting such things, because Brett wasn't out of treatment two weeks before he and Deanna were married in a quiet, private ceremony at a Green Bay church.

In fact, Deanna had been happier than she even imagined possible before the actual wedding. During a visit to Irvin and Bonita Favre's home in mid-May — less than a week into Brett's six-week treatment program — Deanna was joyful, upbeat, almost jolly. Just a few days prior to that, *Sports Illustrated* writer Peter King had been in Gulfport for the first annual Brett Favre Celebrity Golf Tournament and Deanna told him, "A couple of years ago, Brett told me he wanted to be the best quarterback in the NFL. He committed himself to it, and he did it. He'll commit himself to this (recovery from the Vicodin addiction). He knows his career and his life are at stake.

"You know, he's changed already. He talks to me again. He takes Brittany and me out. A few days ago, he hugged me and he thanked me for everything I've done, and he said some really nice things to me. I said, 'I can't believe it. The old Brett's back!' "

Whatever happens on the football field, marriage almost certainly will improve the quality of Favre's life. The tough-as-nails quarterback at last came to the realization that the woman closest to him — whom it's fair to say he took for granted for quite awhile — was not only his best pal but his staunchest ally for the long, tough road ahead.

At the post-treatment press conference, a reporter asked Brett about Deanna's role in his confronting the drug dependency and reaching out for a serious lifestyle change. Favre responded with the predictable response of a happy new bridegroom, and when someone else asked if the couple planned a honeymoon — training camp was due to start a day later — Favre smiled and said, "We've been honeymooning for 12 years already."

However it goes in the won-lost column for Favre and the Packers over the next few seasons, it's obvious that Brett's future is even brighter now than it was when he was throwing 38 touchdown passes and winning the league's MVP award in 1995. He's now a great football player with a complete life.

"I don't want to just get this (drug episode) behind me to get back playing football," Favre said. "I want to be a better person, for my family and friends. That's an area where I definitely could have been better."

On the playing field itself, it's hard to imagine anyone in the NFL with a brighter future.

Just a couple of months prior to Favre's admission of drug dependency and the subsequent treatment, Holmgren was discussing his quarterback's ascendancy to superstar status. "There's no question he's a better player now than he was a couple of years ago," Holmgren said. "He's been in the league long enough that he understands the offense now and he's seen all the different defenses. His reads are better and quicker, his understanding of what to do and when is much more efficient.

"I've worked with Joe Montana and Steve Young and some other great quarterbacks, and Brett has the ability and the work ethic to be as good as any of them. But you know, there is still the possibility that this kid could blow it. He really could. If he starts thinking he knows everything, or that nothing can stop him and he doesn't need to listen to anybody, he could still go backwards.

"I don't want to sound pessimistic, because I'm not. I wouldn't trade Brett Favre for any player in this league. But there's still the danger out there, the possibility that he could take it in the wrong direction. Barring that, or a serious injury, he can be one of the best who ever played."

Holmgren may have been an unknowing prophet. He has insisted he didn't know about Favre's Vicodin woes until just before the official announcement, so you have to assume his warnings weren't about painkillers. The coach was just taking a hard look at his 26-year old hero and cautioning that any one of a number of things might yet derail a brilliant career.

How ironic that Favre's wake-up call – the slap in the face reminding him that neither pro football nor the hard-

Mike Holmgren's relationship with Favre has never been better, and both men understand they'll need each other if their dreams are going to be realized in Green Bay.

knockin' game of life was quite the trip down Easy Street – came when all those awards were arriving by the truckload.

And now one of Holmgren's concerns — that Brett would think the whole thing was just too easy — has been alleviated, albeit by a circumstance nobody wanted to see. However it came about, though, Favre's quick crash back to the real world almost surely will help him in his quest to be an even better quarterback.

For one thing, Brett's Packer teammates have rallied around him as never before — and they were his unflinching allies beforehand. "Whatever it takes to help him, that's what it's going to be," Chmura said. "Everybody on this team is fighting with Brett and for Brett."

Fans have been equally supportive. When the news of Favre's addiction first broke, people like Irvin Favre and Bus Cook, Brett's agent, fretted publicly that Brett might be lumped into a celebrity-turned-junkie heap with such recently defrocked heroes as Bam Morris and Michael Irvin.

"That would really bother me," Irvin said. "Brett hasn't done any illegal dope or anything like that. He took prescription medicine and, yeah, it got to be too much for him. But he wasn't like these other guys who are fooling with cocaine and that stuff. Brett stepped forward, even when he didn't have to, and admitted what was going on so he could help other players and other people with the same kind of problem.

"I don't want to see my son tossed into stories with guys like Irvin and others who have gone out and broken the law and tried all those stupid things just because they're stars and they think they can get away with it. I know I sound like a father, but I truly believe Brett's situation is completely different, and I hope people see it that way."

They have.

Fan support in Green Bay has been predictably overwhelming. At the Packers' first 1996 exhibition game, Favre was cheered until it seemed Lambeau Field might rock on its historic foundations.

But the real surprise was the understanding that apparently flowed out from every other corner of the country. Even flinty-eyed businessmen who make a living on trading cards and other sports memorabilia noted immediately that while the value of Irvin-related items was dropping, Favre's popularity didn't seem to be taking any hit at all.

Favre no doubt was glad to hear things like that, but the funny part is that — for an extremely marketable star — he really isn't much into the endorsement game. Brett doesn't mind doing a card show here and there, or the occasional appearance for friends around Wisconsin and Mississippi, but he'd rather concentrate on football than turn himself into a walking money machine.

Asked point-blank if he'd be cashing in on a lot more opportunities by using a nationally known agent instead of his pal Cook, a Hattiesburg lawyer, Favre responded: "I don't think so. Maybe I could do one or two other things. What they couldn't give me, what Bus and I have, is friendship. Elway told me he never can find Marvin (Demoff) when he wants to talk to him.

Favre has flirted with concussions and other injuries, and now the coaching staff will be watching him more closely than ever.

"Bus doesn't do endorsements for me. If I was in L.A. or New York, playing the way I've played, a lot of endorsements would be coming my way. But I'm much happier here in Green Bay. I don't like shooting commercials. I don't like doing radio spots. But I want people to know who Brett Favre is and how good he is. You've got to win and play well in Green Bay. If not, who wants to market a guy from Green Bay?"

If that sounds like Brett Favre's chosen path to fame and fortune is simply to return the Super Bowl trophy to Green Bay, well, that's because it is. No more, no less.

Packer fans who worry that Brett will bolt for brighter lights when his contract expires after the 1998 season probably have little to fear.

"I've already talked to Ron Wolf (Packer GM) about staying here for the remainder of my career," Favre said. "I'm hoping we can get something done so we don't have to go through what we went through the last time (when Favre was a designated franchise player signed to an offer sheet by New Orleans).

"If we start negotiating now, maybe in a year or two we'll have it done. I want to stay here as long as Ron and Mike and the guys that are here are staying. I'd hate for everyone else to be washed out and have me stay by myself, like General Custer."

Not likely.

Wolf makes that point crystal clear. "Within the bounds of sanity, this organization will do everything necessary to keep Brett Favre here," he said. "He's the guy we've built

Brett Favre: Super Bowl bound?

photo by Vernon Biever

our future around, the guy we think will take this great franchise back to the mountaintop. We owe it to Green Bay to hang on to Brett. He should be a Packer for life. And believe me, I don't want to be remembered as the general manager who let Brett Favre leave town."

The Packers and Favre truly seem like a perfect match. The weather might be a lot different from southern Mississippi to central Wisconsin, but the small-town values and attitudes that Brett has carried all his life are remarkably similar, and he's very comfortable with that.

"Besides, these fans are the kind who appreciate the way I play," Favre said. "They're basically hard-working people who know their football and want to see you play hard and lay it on the line. And that's me, all the way. I think our fans know that, that I'll jump off the top of the stadium if I'd land in the end zone and get us to the Super Bowl.

"I've basically promised everybody that we're going to get there, and I want to keep that promise, whether it's this season or the next one or whenever. We'll get there. Green Bay deserves it. America would love it."

So all that remains in the dreams of the kid from Rotten Bayou, it appears, is winning that biggest game of all for the Green Bay Packers. Oh, and maybe fitting in a delayed honeymoon with Deanna.

Is there a such a thing as the bridal suite at the Super Bowl?